More Praise From Career Professionals:

"In today's constantly changing economy and workplace, knowing how to manage your career successfully is essential. In this book, Koonce provides a combination of unique and timeless advice that's of value to students and mid-career professionals alike."
—Patricia van der Vorm, Executive Director
The Career Center, The American University

"Want to learn how to manage your career more effectively in today's turbulent world? Buy this book. It provides commentary on today's radically new workplace, as well as motivation to become hands-on with your career in ways you've never seen before. This is must-reading for anyone wanting to take control over their work life!"
—Annabelle Reitman, President, American Society for Training
and Development
Washington, D.C. Chapter

"Job hunting is never easy, even in the best of times. Nowadays it can be especially challenging. This book, however, can make your job search or exploration of new career directions a lot easier. Not only is it filled with inspiring examples of people in transition, it will provide you with valuable tools, techniques, and tactics to use in penetrating the hidden job market. And that's where the best jobs, in this or any economy, are to be found."
—Sally Watson, Director of M.B.A. Career Employee
Development, Graduate School of Business
College of William and Mary

"In today's world of diminished job security, people need to think about taking charge of their job and career in ways that were unnecessary a few years ago. *Career Power!* contains state-of-the-art career management advice useful to anyone interested in keeping themselves marketable and attractive to employers in the 21st century. Moreover, it's a fun book to read: full of numerous examples of people in job and career transition who

are actively creating new and exciting career options for themselves. This book is a winner!"
—Joan Strewler, President, Career Dynamics; President, International Association of Career Management Professionals

"Wonderful, contemporary advice on how to take charge of your career from somebody I consider a pro. Trust Richard Koonce! He knows the world of work inside and out. Here's a book you're going to want to keep in your briefcase for ready reference!"
—Madge Kaplan, Boston Bureau Chief, "Marketplace" on American Public Radio

"Whether you're an association executive, salesperson, entrepreneur, or corporate manager, this book does a very nice job of highlighting the things any professional needs to do to be successful in his or her career today. I recommend it highly!"
—Judy Bean, Director of Executive Employment and Career Services, Chicago Society of Association Executives

"This is one of those important books—the ones that can save your life—economically speaking! Koonce was a hot guest on my show and kept the phones buzzing."
—Maggie Moore, Host of "The Maggie Moore Show" on WSPD Radio in Toledo, Ohio

"By breaking traditional paradigms, Richard Koonce, reveals wonderfully refreshing insights into how to achieve personal career goals. His sound advice and pithy style make this must-reading for job seekers and counselors alike."
—David Bacharach, President, Career Search

CAREER POWER!

12
Winning Habits to Get You From Where You Are to Where You Want to Be

Richard Koonce

amacom

American Management Association
New York • Atlanta • Boston • Chicago • Kansas City • San Francisco • Washington, D.C.
Brussels • Mexico City • Tokyo • Toronto

This book is available at a special discount when ordered in bulk quantities. For information, contact Special Sales Department, AMACOM, a division of American Management Association, 135 West 50th Street, New York, NY 10020.

This publication is designed to provide accurate and authoritative information in regard to the subject matter covered. It is sold with the understanding that the publisher is not engaged in rendering legal, accounting, or other professional service. If legal advice or other expert assistance is required, the services of a competent professional person should be sought.

Library of Congress Cataloging-in-Publication Data

Koonce, Richard.
    Career power! : 12 winning habits to get you from where you are to where you want to be / Richard Koonce.
       p. cm.
    Includes bibliographical references and index.
    ISBN 0-8144-7864-6
    1. Vocational guidance.   2. Career development.   I. Title.
HF5381.K634   1994
650.14—dc20   94-29689
                                                                                                                                                            CIP

© 1994 Richard Koonce.
All rights reserved.
Printed in the United States of America.

This publication may not be reproduced,
stored in a retrieval system,
or transmitted in whole or in part,
in any form or by any means, electronic,
mechanical, photocopying, recording, or otherwise,
without the prior written permission of AMACOM,
a division of American Management Association,
135 West 50th Street, New York, NY 10020.

Printing number

10 9 8 7 6 5 4 3 2 1

To **Jack**—

Who said it would all come together one day.
Your friendship is eternal.

And to **Trish**—

Who has helped me get it together these past five years.
What would I do without you? I am so grateful!

Contents

Acknowledgments	*ix*
Introduction: Living a Life of Quiet Desperation at Work?	*xi*
HABIT # 1: Take Responsibility for Managing Your Career	1
HABIT # 2: Define What the Word *Success* Means to You	17
HABIT # 3: Learn How to Transfer Your Skills and Leverage Your Experience	30
HABIT # 4: Develop a Vision of the Future and an Action Plan to Get You There	46
HABIT # 5: Learn to Work "Smart" Where You Are Right Now	61
HABIT # 6: Always Be Prepared for the External Job Market	78
HABIT # 7: Learn to Generate, Explore, and Play With Job Options	89
HABIT # 8: Understand the Power of Other People to Help You Get From Where You Are to Where You Want to Go	105
HABIT # 9: When in Doubt, Invent or Reinvent Yourself!	122
HABIT #10: Master the Art of Graceful Change	129

HABIT #11: Commit Yourself to Lifelong Learning	**138**
HABIT #12: Cultivate Emotional and Psychological Heartiness	**152**
References and Suggested Reading	*161*
Index	*165*

Acknowledgments

One of my cardinal beliefs about job hunting and career planning is that none of us achieves the worthwhile things of life alone. Indeed, a large part of life involves learning to accept the help, guidance, and loving emotional support of other people along the way.

I certainly came to know the importance of this belief as I wrote this book. Many people contributed to its writing, by giving of their time for interviews, by reviewing early drafts, or by being there, late at night or early in the morning, with a cheerful word or hearty embrace to fortify me for the task of completing and then polishing the manuscript. Writing is nothing if not "the labor of the file," and I'm deeply grateful to all of those in my family of friends and dear ones who have supported me in this endeavor.

There are too many people to thank individually, but I want to cite those who played a particularly important role in helping me write this book. Please know that each of you is special to me, for the time and the talent that you have given to make it possible.

To Cheryl Meyer Iskandar, John Barth, Matt Whalen, and Mary Crannell, all of whom gave generously of their time to review and edit my manuscript—you had your work cut out for you as you gallantly strived to cut it down to a manageable size! Many thanks for your comments and suggestions about how to tighten things up.

To Mary Jettner and Susan Walker, both of whom put in long hours after their work days were over to transcribe interviews and to help me learn Wordperfect—I have now learned how important it is to save documents in a backup file!

To Mary and Bill Marsden, John Galligan, and Merphil Kondo—you folks were there to pick me up off the floor the day my computer crashed. For your generosity I will always be grateful. You are true friends, and I owe you all dinner.

To Nina Graybill, my agent—you helped me craft a few random ideas into the manuscript that eventually became this book.

To my colleagues at EnterChange and Manchester—you are first-class. Your wisdom, knowledge, and insight about the changing nature of the workplace enriched the text of this book in myriad ways.

To other friends and colleagues, including Jane Shore, Mort Cohen, David Bauer, Annabelle Reitman, Norma Opgrand, Larry Lane, Jim Walker, Leslie Shields, John Carroll, Dave Coleman, Rick Dillon, Ken Einhaus, Kevin Nourse, Jeff Jorney, Joan Strewler, Susan Flagler, Bob Morgan, Charles Cates, Curt Culhane, Linda Penrod, Dennis Wholey, Clinton Anderson, and Joan Beilstein—your specific comments subtly influenced the tone and writing of this book.

Finally, to all the people in job and career transition with whom I've had the pleasure to work over the years—you've taught me all I know and enabled me to share your wisdom with others.

Much of the material that appears in this book first appeared in the form of radio essays that aired on American Public Radio's *Marketplace*, heard on public radio stations across the United States. I am indebted to John Barth and his colleagues at *Marketplace*. You are a great group of people to work with!

Introduction: Living a Life of Quiet Desperation at Work?

Years ago, I worked for a large *Fortune* 100 company on the executive staff of a regional vice president. While most of the people in this organization filled the bill as "buttoned-down" Wharton Business School types, there was also a somewhat rumpled and irreverent Italian guy on staff named Tony.

Tony looked like the kind of guy who might well have walked in off the set of "Roseanne" or been one of Archie Bunker's loading-dock buddies on "All in the Family." Had he not been responsible for our computer and telephone operations, Tony would have been perfectly happy pumping gas somewhere or flipping burgers at Burger King, spending his off-hours listening to Tina Turner and drinking Iron City beer.

Indeed, by his own admission, Tony was a "salt-of-the-earth guy with an ample girth" who, though he wore the same blue pinstripes as everybody else in the office (*Dress for Success* was required company reading at the time), just didn't look the part. Yet Tony had an insight into other people that I have encountered only a few times in my life.

"You don't fit in around here," he once told me. "You stick out like a sore thumb."

"What do you mean?" I asked, a bit irritated but also intrigued by his comment. I knew I might well have asked him the same question.

"You know what I mean," he said between drags on a cigarette. "You like to write, you like to work with people. So why are you wasting your time and talents here, grinding out corporate paperwork and pushing budget reports around in the catacombs of this organization?"

I've never forgotten Tony's insightful words. Indeed, he's the one who's largely responsible for my eventually hearing my "vocational voice"—the voice that even back then was whispering to me that I was in the wrong place and that I wasn't doing the right things with my life.

And yet it took me three years before I acted on Tony's advice, got out of the job I was in, and segued into something more meaningful. Instead, I stayed put, plateaued and pigeon-holed, in an organization that just didn't know what to do with me. I lived a life of "quiet desperation" at work—until, as the saying goes, "I got sick and tired of being sick and tired" about my career.

The dilemma I faced back then may be what you're facing today. Perhaps you're stuck in a job you don't like, one that doesn't use your skills and talents to their fullest—but you don't know what to do. Or perhaps you like what you're doing for a living but are wondering what comes next and how you get there. Or perhaps you're desperate to get out of where you are and do something else but feel trapped because you've put in so many years toward retirement.

Believe me, you have options. And there is hope!

That's why I wrote this book.

Today, I am in a very good place. I got out of that large corporation that didn't know what to do with me, started my own business, and put in time along the way as a consultant to a variety of *Fortune* 100 companies—among them the one where I'd been so miserable as a full-time employee.

Today I have more business options than I could ever have imagined. I'm more financially successful than I would have been had I stayed put in that old corporate job. And I have done things—like write this book, be a monthly magazine columnist, and appear on radio and television—that I probably wouldn't have been able to do had I stayed "narrowly niched" and in a tight little box on somebody else's organization chart.

But one thing is clear: You can't move—upwards and onwards (or even sideways for that matter) with your career—without a strong commitment to and a belief in yourself and without learning some new tactics and strategies to help you navigate through the whitewater of today's turbulent economy and uncertain job market.

Indeed, you need a new kind of career compass and roadmap to help you plot and chart your career course in the years ahead.

What's more, you need to eliminate any excuses that you may tend to bring up every time you start thinking more proactively about managing your career. In other words, commit yourself, as of this moment, to the goal of taking charge of planning and managing your career successfully in the years ahead. Don't let yourself get thrown off stride, as I sometimes say, "by every hangnail and pistachio shell that happens to cross your path!"

I developed *Career Power!* after years of working with people in job and career transition. As you'll find, we're not talking here about anything as abstruse as physics or organic chemistry. Career planning isn't brain surgery or rocket science. It's more in the nature of common sense—like knowing enough to pay attention to your investments, shop around for the best health care coverage for your family, or practice safer sex. You need common sense when it comes to managing your career for a very simple reason: The old rules of employment (e.g., job security and "womb-to-tomb" employment) just don't apply anymore. As a consequence, you must be purposeful about enhancing your job security and marketability on an ongoing basis, at the same time fending off potential professional obsolescence that can creep up on any professional.

Throughout this book there are simple exercises to help you focus your thinking and direct your energy to the task of managing your career and developing new options and opportunities for yourself. Many of us practice limiting thinking about our careers. Yet chances are excellent, if you're reading this book, that you have more going for you than you realize. But the first and hardest person to convince of that may be not a boss or a prospective new employer—but you yourself!

Take the "twelve habits of career success" to heart. They're intended to be a career planning system that can help you evaluate your career on an ongoing basis and take steps to move toward new career goals.

Despite what you hear on radio and TV or what you may read in newspapers and magazines, there are new and exciting opportunities out there for you, even in today's economy. So how do you grab them? In many cases, it takes new approaches to exploring the job market. It also requires a willingness to "break out of the box that may be your current frame of reference"—about work and about yourself. You might, for instance, be able to "co-create" a job with an employer or find "back" and "side" doors into organizations by positioning yourself with the right people.

This book is designed to help you by equipping you with new ways to think about work and your career. It isn't about job hunting per se. Instead, it's intended to be a tactical and strategic career planning guide that you can use throughout your working life.

If you don't like where you're working or what you're doing, it's important to listen to your feelings and devise a plan of escape—a way to move on to something (or segue into something) that represents a better professional fit and that will be more meaningful and rewarding.

Throughout this book you'll meet a lot of people in job and career transition. While each is a real person, I have fictionalized their stories in some cases or changed certain details to preserve anonymity. I am indebted to each of them for their generosity and time in talking with me as I wrote this book.

As you read *Career Power!*, I would welcome your ideas and comments. Perhaps you've been through a significant job or career transition in your own life and have an interesting anecdote to share. I would welcome hearing from you. You're welcome to contact me care of AMACOM Books.

Your work is to discover your work and then with all your heart to give yourself to it.

—Buddha

Choose a job you love, and you will never have to work a day in your life.

—Confucius

CAREER POWER!

HABIT #1

Take Responsibility for Managing Your Career

> The very best way to relate to our work is to choose it. Unfortunately, since we learn early to act on what others say, value and expect, we often find ourselves a long way down the wrong road before realizing we did not actually choose our work. Turning our lives around is usually the beginning of maturity since it means correcting choices made unconsciously, without deliberation or thought.
>
> —Marsha Sinetar
> *Do What You Love, The Money Will Follow*

Eleven thousand days of our lives!

Roughly speaking, that's the amount of time we spend at work between the ages of twenty-one and sixty-five. It's a staggering amount of time to commit to any single activity. Have you planned carefully to make the most of your career? What do you want from your career, other than a steady paycheck and a secure retirement? Professional recognition, the respect of coworkers, an equity position in your own business, or just the opportunity to collect a gold watch?

Ironically, even in what author Warren Bennis has called the "age of the manager," the notion of actively managing one's career is still something of an alien notion to many people. Surprisingly, the idea of actually putting together a career plan based on our interests, abilities, and passions is something most of us have never considered doing. Yet in today's volatile business climate, actively planning and managing a career has never been more important.

Mergers, acquisitions, downsizings, and corporate restructurings continue to be a way of life in the American workplace. At the same time, emerging technologies, the push toward a global economy, and the need for businesses to compete more productively are all rewriting the rules of the American workplace. These trends are fundamentally changing the nature of the implicit (in some cases, explicit) psychological contract that has long existed between companies and their employees.

While this book isn't about the changing workplace as such, it is about how you need to react to those changes effectively and to develop "response-ability" if you want to enhance your job security and professional marketability.

The New Workplace Ground Rules

- *Today, of course, you can't be sure that your job is secure.* There are very few (if any) safe harbors of employment (including jobs in state and federal government), and companies that once tacitly touted "womb-to-tomb" employment, such as the phone company, don't do so anymore.

- *Change has become the one constant in the modern workplace.* Indeed, one of the "core competencies" you need to develop to succeed professionally today is the ability to manage both the stresses and the tasks associated with ongoing workplace and organizational change.

- *Our economy isn't dying or stagnating as some claim. Instead, it is in a constant state of reconfiguring itself.* This is apparent by the continuing transformation of many industries (e.g., defense and telecommunications) and the strong emergence and growth of others (e.g., healthcare, environmental waste management, biotech, software development, and information management and movement). If you can begin to anticipate changes, discern trends, and predict business needs, you can make shrewd career moves that will consistently keep you ahead of the change curve and enable you to position yourself for professional opportunities.

- *Your continuing employment will increasingly be linked to short-term job performance, the currency and relevancy of your skills to your employer's core business, and the impact of your contribution to your organization's bottom line.* Many organizations are moving toward having smaller core workforces. In these organizations the work of core employees is being supplemented by contract workers, part-timers, and consultants paid for their subject matter expertise and participation in specific projects.

- *Even in companies that continue to hire and retain workers, traditional career paths are often nonexistent today, and lean organizational structures present fewer opportunities for upward mobility.* Given this reality, you'll need to think of new ways to grow and develop professionally.

- *You must treat your "skill-set"—your specific bag of skills, talents, and experience—as a rare asset.* It's a professional nest-egg! This asset will need to be carefully nurtured over time if you wish to use it as a solid foundation for future success. If you fail to do this, your skill-set will become dated, outmoded, and eventually ill-suited to your organization's changing needs.

- *It will be up to you, not your employer, to keep your skills and expertise up to date.* You will feel subtle or direct pressure to do this as technological advances drive workplace change, as jobs are redesigned or eliminated, and as your employer continuously evaluates you on the basis of the "value-added" contribution you make at work.

- *Many employers give abundant lip service to the idea that employees are "their greatest asset," but few employers actually put their money where their mouth is.* For this reason, don't look for employers to earmark copious amounts of corporate cash to help develop you as an employee. While this is unfortunate (and extremely shortsighted from a management viewpoint), it needn't stop you from pursuing your own ongoing professional development.

- *Recognize that the U.S. economy has become a crazy quilt of job and employment arrangements, only one of which is permanent, full-time employmen with a single employer.* "Borderless" jobs (working across geographical borders and international time zones) and "virtual" work options (working from virtually anywhere, anytime) are two of the newest job options. They are joining already well-established alternatives to permanent, full-time employment, including contractual, consultative, and interim employment arrangements, as well as part-time, flex-time, telecommuting, and job-sharing options.

While many of these options afford tremendous flexibility—especially for people who have daycare or eldercare concerns to think about, for example—they also pose unique challenges when it comes to planning for retirement, health-care coverage, or even the guarantee of workplace rights. Federal equal employment opportunity protection, for example, does not extend to independent contractors.

Answering a Wake-Up Call to Us All

Given the ground rules operating in the American workplace, it's critical that you take active control of your career as you never had to do in the past. Increasingly, it will be up to you to chart where you want to go professionally without the benefit of mentoring bosses, benevolent organizations, generous employee benefit packages, and paternalistic corporate philosophies.

This is not to say that you won't be able to find help and guidance from other people throughout the course of your career. On the other hand, you can't afford to crouch behind your desk, bury your head in your work, defer your career plans to your boss, or assume that by being a "good employee" you will ensure your job security. You won't.

The best way to stay employed, today and in the future, is to look upon yourself as being in business for yourself. In other words, put the onus for job security on your own shoulders and know which of your skills you can easily take someplace else and what you can do to keep your skills in "state-of-the-art" condition.

Later in this chapter, I outline some "fast-start" ways for you to take responsibility for managing your career. But first, let's look at why a lot of people never take firm control of their professional circumstances.

Reason #1: We Don't Feel Entitled to or Capable of a Better Career

When we think seriously about what we'd really like to be doing for a living, we may hear a nagging little voice inside of us saying, "That's foolish. You'll never go anywhere with that idea!" or "That's unrealistic. Wake up and smell the coffee!"

Most people walk around with negative "narrators" inside their heads—at least some of the time. This narrator speaks in many voices, often telling people they can't succeed or get ahead in life. My friend and colleague Richard Carson refers to these voices as the "gremlins" of human existence, trying at every turn to thwart your happiness. Indeed, he's written a wonderful book on the subject titled *Taming Your Gremlin: A Guide to Enjoying Yourself.*

In a sense, the little voices that speak up inside your head when it comes to your career are those of your "career gremlins." Your career gremlins use fear to manipulate and disempower you. They try to convince you that whatever it is you want from your job and your professional life, you can't have, don't deserve, couldn't possibly attain, and wouldn't really want it even if you got it.

Your gremlins do this, of course, under the guise of reasonableness and common sense. They can seem very seductive and logical as they undermine your self-confidence, encourage you to live in denial, warn you against taking any risks, and thereby keep you from making personal or professional progress in your life.

"Don't take chances," one career gremlin will argue.

"Why don't you just relax, kick back, and wait to collect your retirement check?" another will say.

"Your job's safe; you don't need to worry! You'll have this job forever," a third will chime in.

The bottom line is this: You need to know the ways in which your career gremlins operate, lest they keep you from doing things in your life that you really want to do.

Reason #2: We Get "Distracted by Elvis"

Perhaps you're not plagued by self-doubts when it comes to your career. Perhaps instead you suffer from the common human predilection to procrastinate and dither.

Do you tend to put off until tomorrow job and career tasks you should have done today or even last year? Like exhuming that résumé? You may decide that before you sit down and think about your career, you've got to:

- Pay this month's bills.
- Do the laundry.
- Mow the grass.
- Plan that holiday dinner for the family.
- Get the kids signed up for soccer or Little League.
- Clean out the garage.
- Repanel the family room.
- Dust.
- Catch your favorite episode of *Gilligan's Island* on cable for the forty-eighth time.

Stay on this course, and you'll be in your grave long before you've taken a single step forward with your career. As success coach Tony Robbins suggests, "Don't major in minor things; think BIG!"

A lot of people procrastinate when it comes to thinking about their careers. I call this the phenomenon of "getting distracted by Elvis." Here's why:

Millions of people in this country are obsessed with Elvis. They invest copious amounts of time and energy speculating about whether he's really dead or is in fact alive and well and working in a convenience store somewhere. Who cares?

As far as I know, Elvis is dead and will be for a long time, which makes wasting your energy ruminating about whether he is among us a colossal nonissue. Yet the Elvis question is illustrative of how a lot of us invest time and energy in things outside our zone of control or on things that have no meaningful or practical consequence for us as individuals.

We do this because we find it easier and more fun to focus on, worry about, and complain about things outside ourselves than on the reality and challenges of living our own lives.

I'm convinced that this is why many of us become so addicted to soap operas and daytime talk shows. It's easier to dwell on other people's lives and problems than it is to focus on our own trials and travails.

Now, don't get me wrong. I'm not bashing Elvis. Or even daytime TV. Healthy diversions are important.

But if you get "distracted by Elvis" on a regular basis, you'll never do anything significant about managing your career—or much else of import. Henry David Thoreau once took note of the human inclination to wander from the larger tasks of life when he wrote, "Let us spend one day as deliberately as nature, and not be thrown off the track by every nutshell and mosquito's wing that falls on the rails."

Reason #3: We're Still Trying to Please Our Parents, Our Teachers, Our Coaches, or Somebody Else, Rather Than Ourselves

This is an extremely common career roadblock, which plagues a lot of people. My grandfather is a case in point. Years ago he was a popular minister in the Presbyterian Church. Indeed, he was beloved by the people he served, first as a missionary in the Alaska Yukon and then in pastorates in Florida and Ohio.

But being a minister wasn't what Martin Egbert Koonce wanted for himself. His mother chose that calling for him, and so he remained dissatisfied with his career for the bulk of his life. He really wanted to be an engineer.

Then there's the case of "Lloyd," with whom I worked last year. A talented surgeon, Lloyd yearned for years to get out of medicine. He wanted very much to move into nonprofit work, ideally to become an association executive or health-care administrator, and to work in a team setting—something he feels he couldn't do in the hierarchically oriented world of medicine.

Lloyd is fortunate in one respect. He already has most of the formal credentials necessary to make a transition into another career. He has, for example, served on the boards of numerous health-related organizations and agencies, been deeply involved in medical task-force work, and acquired a master's degree in administrative services from a well-respected university.

So, what's been stopping Lloyd, the talented, educated surgeon, from embarking on a career that will make him happier? His parents and their expectations. Sound familiar?

Lloyd's father was a prominent surgeon and his mother an extremely strong influence in his early life. Lloyd has had to battle a sense of shame, guilt, and anxiety as he's thought about pursuing a career other than medicine. This is true even today, although he is in his early fifties and his mother is in her eighties.

"My mother had professions picked out for both me and my brother," Lloyd recalls. "My assignment was to follow in my father's footsteps and become this city's second premier surgeon, following behind him. That is still her expectation, although it has never been mine."

Lloyd remembers vividly how his mother tried to impose that career choice on him even when he was a child. "Whenever I made a decision she didn't approve of, her famous phrase was 'Do you think that's wise?'" he says. There was also a "very unexpressed—but very palpable—withdrawal of approval, love, and acceptance if I persisted in my choices about things," he says.

Today, Lloyd is shifting out of medicine, but it has been difficult. He grew up lacking a sense of confidence about making his own decisions, while hungering for external validation that came only in the form of conditional love from his mother. "I think two of the major issues in my career have been a need for external validation and the feeling that either an outside authority or higher authority always had a veto power over my decisions," he says.

From years of working with people in job and career transition, I've observed that, like Lloyd, many adults continue to be dominated and ruled by parental injunctions or "family scripts" that they internalized as kids. These things often limit how people look at the world and themselves.

Author Rozelle Lerner sheds important light on the ways that the early adoption of negative or limiting "family scripts" keeps us from trusting our gut when it comes to making adult choices:

> As a child, I was taught not to think for myself, not to trust or value my own inner voice. My parents fostered

dependence and I discounted my own wisdom. I came to rely exclusively on others' input for my decisions. As I grew into adulthood, I silenced my intuition altogether, and, as a result, made many poor decisions that caused me pain. I have since learned from my mistakes, and have at last come to trust the wisdom of my inner voice.[1]

When it comes to your career, whom are you trying to please? Is it you or somebody else? The entertainer Fanny Brice once said, "Let the world know you as you are, not as you think you should be, because sooner or later, if you are posing, you will forget the pose, and then where are you?"

Reason #4: We "Parentify" Our Employers

Do you tend to think of your boss as a surrogate mother or father figure? As somebody who knows what's best for you in your career?

Until a few years ago, the rules of the employment game often encouraged the development of dependent "parent-child" relationships between bosses and their subordinates. This was often an implicit basis of the reporting relationships between bosses and their subordinates in corporate America. "Womb-to-tomb" employment was an unstated presumption when a person came to work, and being "a good and loyal employee" was often as highly valued as the skills and abilities a person could bring to the job.

In some cases, we unconsciously seek out in our relationships with bosses patterns that mirror the kind of relationships we had with our parents or with other authority figures when we were growing up.

"Roland" is a good example. He's a thirty-six-year-old social worker who feels that on at least four occasions in his career he has "parentified" his boss. As the child of an alcoholic, he acknowledges that he had a role in "co-creating" unfortunate and unsatisfying relationships with bosses, relationships in which he often felt treated like a child and that were typified by a lack of communication and occasional emotional and verbal haranguing and abuse.

"I think it's very easy for anyone who comes out of a dysfunctional or codependent family background to get sucked into this dynamic without even being consciously aware of it," he says. "It feels familiar to you, and people may even think they need to do it to get ahead in their organization."

---

1. Rozelle Lerner, *Affirmations for the Inner Child* (Deerfield Beach, Fla.: Health Communications Inc., 1990), p. 18.

It's not uncommon for people unconsciously to develop parent-child relationships with their bosses, so be careful. If you like to please other people, want to fit in, and like to be liked, you can easily fall prey to this syndrome. And there are more than a few bosses out there who, out of either their own insecurity or emotional immaturity, still crave this kind of relationship with their subordinates.

Reason #5: We Affirm Self-Limitations

Unfortunately, a lot of people believe there's nothing they can do to improve their professional circumstances and that true professional success is meant for somebody else. People like this discount their ability to make things happen. As the psychologist Rollo May has observed, "Many people feel they are powerless to do anything effective with their lives. It takes courage to break out of the settled mold [so] most find conformity more comfortable. This is why the opposite of courage in our society is not cowardice—it's conformity."

Recognizing Emotional and Psychological Hurdles

If you tend to doubt your ability to cope with life, there's a good chance that you have created excuses or emotional and psychological barriers that keep you from pursuing what you want.

Do any of these messages sound familiar?

"I'm not special enough to really succeed." Think you're not good enough or special enough to succeed? A lot of geniuses throughout history appeared to have little initial potential. Many never stood out in school. Albert Einstein, for one, was a terrible critic of the school system of his day, because it labeled him as having little potential. Yet by the time he was twenty-six years old, Einstein had already produced an amount of research work that, as astronomer Carl Sagan notes, would have represented "an impressive output for any other physicist over an entire lifetime."

"I don't have the education I need." Consider these facts: Bill Lear, inventor of the Learjet, the first car radio, and the first eight-track stereo system, was a ninth-grade dropout; the late Dizzy Gillespie, the famed trumpeter who died in 1993, never had a trumpet lesson. Steve Jobs, founder of Apple Computer and creator of the personal computer, was a college dropout, as was Tom Managhan, the founder of Domino's Pizza; ABC anchorman Peter Jennings also never completed college.

"I'm too old to succeed." Maybe you think that it's too late for you to embark on a successful new career, that you're over the hill, that you have nothing special to offer at your age. But consider this: Grandma Moses didn't start painting until she was in her seventies. Famed supermodel Lauren Hutton's career took off and found new life when she turned fifty—an age at which it used to be assumed a model's career was over. And writer James Michener, who has written forty books in his lifetime, completed *Mexico* in 1992 at age 86!

"I'm too young to succeed in that field." Maybe your concern isn't that you feel too old to succeed but that you think you're too young, that nobody will take you seriously. If you begin to feel this way, consider these facts: George Stephanopolous was only thirty-one when he was named Bill Clinton's White House director of communications; success coach, author, and master motivator Tony Robbins was a millionaire by age 24 and is the founder of nine companies; Laura Pederson, author of the book *Street Smart Career Guide,* was only twenty-three when she made her first million on Wall Street.

"I can't get ahead because I'm . . ." You fill in the blank: black, female, handicapped, whatever. Think this is the case? Tell that to General Colin Powell, who in 1993 retired as the first black chairman of the Joint Chiefs of Staff and who is being touted as a potential presidential candidate by both major political parties.

Or tell it to Kevin Robinson, a former forest ranger and avid outdoorsman, who in 1975 suffered a traumatic accident that left him a quadriplegic. Today, Kevin works as a freelance writer and photographer in Kansas City, Kansas. Despite the fact that he has the use of only his left ring finger, Kevin has written and published three novels.

Kevin's story is testimony of how people can overcome even the most devastating of personal circumstances to triumph in life. The same year that he was paralyzed, Kevin's house burned down and he and his family were involved in a terrible van accident that almost killed his wife.

I first became acquainted with Kevin when he called to interview me for an article in *Woman's World* magazine. But I quickly became intrigued by his story. For here is a man who hasn't let anything stand in his way—not even circumstances that would have surely crushed many people.

To what does this man attribute his success and perseverance in life? Being proactive and taking responsibility, he says.

> If an individual is used to being a fighter, as I am, you
> set yourself a goal. I wanted to be active again, I wanted to

get up and be out and doing whatever I could do. That's in my nature. So the bigger the challenge, the busier I am. If you're not doing everything you're capable of doing, you have no right to demand that everybody else around you make your life easier.

Taking Responsibility for Your Career

Okay, you're saying, "What do I do? If all the rules of the workplace and the employment game have changed, how do I take responsibility for my own career choices? How can I overcome my own self-limitations?"

Here's a list of things I suggest you do immediately to help you take greater responsibility for managing your career. These are things that will make you feel more in control of your professional life, and more capable of generating options for yourself:

Taking Control of Your Career

1. *Realize that you are entitled to any job or career in this world for which you are willing to strive and work.* It may require some work, additional education, or patience, but if you've got the gumption and stick-to-itiveness you can accomplish just about anything you want. One key to motivation is feeling you're worthy of something better!

2. *Visualize yourself* TODAY *in the job of your dreams, then focus at least twenty minutes of energy and effort every day on making that dream become reality.* You might want to write down your dream and put it on your refrigerator, on your bathroom mirror, or on the wall in your office. Seeing it each day will help you internalize its message and help you move toward it.

3. *Develop a strategy—solid and clearly stated steps that will help move you toward the job of your dreams.* What career or careers do you want, and what reasonable short-term goals will get you there? Developing strong career goals is the critical underpinning for taking charge of your career.

4. *If you're not sure of exactly what you want next out of your career, give yourself permission to explore some options.* Seek out people you know and trust for advice and assistance. Have faith that in doing so, you will move toward greater awareness of what you want for yourself. Much of the material in the rest of this book is designed to give you the tools to explore job and career options.

5. *Develop an intense desire to achieve your career goal(s) and take note of defining moments or "rites of passage" that represent significant steps for you toward those goals.* What have you done that already significantly marks your progress toward attaining a major job or career goal? Perhaps you've recently completed a college degree, the first person in your family to do so. Or perhaps you've recently acquired a master's degree in your chosen field, a credential you know will help you advance in your career.

Identify, savor, and celebrate moments of success like these. They are mile markers for you on the way to the attainment of longer-term career goals and dreams.

6. *Read the stories of women and men who have succeeded at doing what they wanted to do with their careers.* Their stories will provide you with comfort and confidence in moments when you doubt your ability to achieve what you want for yourself. Keep an "inspiration file" of stories that are especially meaningful to you. Go hear your "heroes" speak, or arrange to meet with them. You may find them more accessible than you imagine.

7. *Understand that feeling a little fear is always a part of taking control of your life and career.* Don't squelch these feelings. Major life changes are unsettling. Acknowledge your fears, then harness them to help you pursue your dreams. Believe in yourself and in the inner voice within you that tells you, "Yes I can achieve what I dream of doing!"

8. *Realize that you are unique both as a human being and as a professional.* You have a right to a meaningful job and career. In this regard, what you think of yourself is the key to your success and happiness. As Harvard psychologist William James once said, "You are what you think about most of the time!"

9. *Don't let anyone tell you what you can and can't have out of a career!* There are those you will meet along the pathway to your next job or career who will question your motives, your dreams, your chances, your intelligence, and your competence. This frequently occurs in the lives of women and minorities, but it can happen to anyone. If it happens, don't let it rattle you. It may be that they are envious of your dreams and impressed by (but threatened by or jealous of) your drive and intelligence. Indeed, as many capable women will attest, a lot of men are threatened by competence in women. Don't despair. Instead, take note of what Eleanor Roosevelt once said about facing down adversity: "I gain strength, courage, and confidence by every experience in which I must stop and look fear in the face. I say to myself, 'I've lived

through this and can take the next thing that comes along.' We must do the things we think we cannot do."

10. *Strive to develop a professional identity that is independent of your job description, title, and organization.* It's an unfortunate fact of professional life that most organizations tend to put their employees "in boxes." At its worst, this can be dehumanizing. Short of that, it can be disempowering—if you buy into being put into a box. (See Exhibit 1-1.)

Nowadays, however, there are numerous ways to break out of the box—to develop a professional identity that is apart from and independent of your job title, position, or function. Consider getting involved in professional groups and associations. Develop a contact network that involves you with peers from other companies and organizations. And strive to become known in your field by presenting seminars and workshops and delivering speeches and talks to outside groups. You might even think about writing a book!

All these things will give you a sense of satisfaction, empowerment, self-confidence, and professional competence that is derived from activities outside your office.

11. *Don't rely on your boss or organization to define your career path or options, or even to understand what you do.* Years ago, especially in large companies, mentoring employees was a standard part of a supervisor's job description. Today, things are often quite different.

Organizations of all sizes and in all industries are dealing with change as never before, and managers spend most of their time managing bottom-line business objectives. There is less time to spend helping subordinates develop their own careers. And in many cases, supervisors aren't comfortable with their ability to mentor others.

12. *Don't let yourself become a job or career victim.* The victim mentality has gained a lot of currency in our culture in recent years. People file lawsuits, tie up the courts, and become litigious at the drop of a hat over all sorts of things when the true issue is often one of personal or professional responsibility.

Of course, there are real victims in this world. But taking on the role of "victim" will not empower you to find or create better professional circumstances. It is far more likely to sap your energy and to delay your entry into other professional arenas that will be more rewarding.

If you feel victimized by your circumstances, you may be working for an abusive boss or a toxic organization that is unable to provide you with a quality working environment. In some cases it will be appropriate to take legal action to resolve difficulties (e.g., sexual harassment), but in other instances (e.g., a layoff or downsizing), weigh carefully the costs and benefits of pursuing litigation.

Exhibit 1-1. The three boxes that organizations put employees in.

Feel boxed in at your job? Feel your boss is unwilling or unable to see or appreciate all the skills and talents you bring to the table?

You're not alone. Organizations often lack the will, competence, presence of mind, or imagination to use you as fully as they might. That can leave you frustrated and your organization shortchanged of the talent at its fingertips.

Even in the best of jobs, you'll probably feel confined occasionally. But there's a difference between feeling that you're outgrowing a job and being forced to fit into a smaller space (or position) than is comfortable.

Employers in general and bosses in particular tend to put people in three different kinds of boxes:

1. THE PLAYPEN

You'll know if your boss has put you in a playpen because he will tend to infantalize you in some way. Typically, in instances like this, you're not valued, acknowledged, or empowered to do more than what the boss specifically asks for. I once worked for a guy who put me in a playpen. He was an insecure, top-down manager who didn't want to interact with me; he simply wanted to delegate tasks to me. Looking back, it appears to me that he was seeking to gain emotional and professional dominion over me. He had a hard time acknowledging my professional competence and initially quibbled with me when I came to work for him about what my title would be. That, in fact, was a red flag that I failed to take note of!

People who are put in playpens often feel victimized and unempowered to change their circumstances.

2. THE JAIL CELL

Even worse than the playpen is the jail cell. If your job is a jail cell, you typically have a lot of responsibility but little or no authority with which to accomplish what is expected of you. In many instances, your job is undoable. Besides having little or no autonomy to get work done, you typically are provided with insufficient resources (e.g., office support, backing by champions within the organization, or budget) to carry out your personal or departmental objectives. Jobs that are jail cells often experience a great deal of turnover because the hiring or supervising manager either can't or won't acknowledge that professional people need both latitude and purview to get their work done efficiently.

3. THE SANDBOX

This is the kind of job to have. If your job is a sandbox, metaphorically speaking, it enables you to combine work, learning, and enjoyment in ways that help you grow and develop professionally. This kind of job is "self-developing"; it is, by definition, a "learning ground" where you can creatively and effectively develop skills and perform to peak levels.

I've had several jobs that were sandboxes. My early jobs in broadcast journalism, for example, enabled me to grow by leaps and bounds. In going out and interviewing people, gathering news, and then producing my own radio reports each day, I learned a tremendous amount about all sorts of things in a brief period of time—from how to interview and splice tape to how to write for broadcast and anchor a newscast.

My job as a trainer and seminar developer with AT&T also provided me with an important learning ground. It was an environment in which I was simultaneously performing my job and discovering new abilities—in my case, as a presenter, trainer, and platform speaker.

---

13. *Come up with some career affirmations to sustain you as you go forward.* Write one to yourself each day on a 3 × 5 card, then post it in a prominent place at home, in the office, or in the car, where you can be reminded of it and commit it to memory.

14. *Finally, be intentional and purposeful about taking charge of your professional life.* It's important that you develop intentionality and "presence of mind" about where you want to go in the years ahead. This will

open up your heart and mind to possibilities and options that you might not otherwise imagine.

At the same time, savor each day as much as you can, and find something—anything—about your daily work that you can enjoy or learn from. You may find that, even in the midst of difficulties, there are good omens pointing you in new and more satisfying directions.

As Napoleon Hill, the famous author and motivational expert, once advised: "Every adversity carries with it the seed of an equivalent or greater benefit."

Resonating with that same thought was George Bernard Shaw, who wrote, "The people who get on in this world are those who get up and look for the circumstances they want, and if they can't find them, they make them."

HABIT #2

Define What the Word *Success* Means to You

> To laugh often and much; to win the respect of intelligent people and affection of children; to earn the appreciation of honest critics and endure the betrayal of false friends; to appreciate beauty; to find the best in others; to leave the world a bit better, whether by a healthy child, a garden patch or a redeemed social condition; to know even one life has breathed easier because you have lived. This is to have succeeded.
>
> —Ralph Waldo Emerson

Americans, more than people in other cultures, tend to define themselves by what they do. If you don't think that's true, just try going to a dinner party and not talking to anybody else about what you do for a living. And while you're at it, don't ask the other guests what they do for a living, either!

You'll probably find yourself at a loss for words and hitting on the onion dip and hot hors d'oeuvres a bit more than usual as you grope for a conversation icebreaker.

Identifying with your work is okay—when it's work you enjoy. But there's a danger when too much of your identity and self-worth become vested in a job title or in a job you don't like. This is something a lot of Americans are prone to.

Defining Success Your Way

As Dr. Steven Berglas notes in his book *The Success Syndrome,* our society tends to value ranking and rewards over the importance of finding personal fulfillment. Does success to you mean having a prestigious job, a big salary, a big house? Or does it mean something else—helping people, being financially independent, working for a nonprofit, or starting your own business?

There's no one definition of success that fits everybody. It's really up to you to define what success and happiness mean to you.

A lot of people don't know this. So they work very hard to adhere to what they think is society's definition of success, and if they don't get it, or don't get it all at once, or don't have it "all together" by age 30 or 40 or 50, they consider themselves failures.

In so doing, they become slaves to the tyranny of other people's expectations. By at least one estimate, four out of five of us don't like what we do for a living, a grim statistic that suggests that Thoreau was right: Most people are living lives of "quiet desperation."

Now don't get me wrong. I have no problem with money, prestige, status, or fame. But what's the point of making $150,000 a year as a lawyer if it means you have to work ninety hours a week to be considered for partner and you'd rather watch your daughter play soccer?

You need to find what in your heart you want—not what society tells you you should want. Avoid a narrow view of what success is supposed to look like.

I used to have a limited view of what professional success really meant. I was raised to believe that for a man, it meant putting on a suit each day, taking the bus or the train into the city, slaving away at a desk in an office for ten to twelve hours, then coming home—only to get back up again and do the very same thing the next morning.

I learned this model from my dad, who did this for years. He enjoyed what he did, but I can't stand the thought of being chained to a desk all day. I need variety, the opportunity to interact with other people, deliver seminars, and, of course, find time to write, be it early in the morning or late at night. Who says you have to bivouacked in an office all day long?

Here are a couple of pointers on redefining success.

- *Give yourself permission to define success for yourself.* There's an old proverb that says, "Do not follow where the road may lead. Go instead where there is no path and leave a trail." Sometimes people just need permission from somebody else to explore a road less traveled.

Maybe someone in your life (your wife, husband, partner, boyfriend, girlfriend, or just a trusted business friend) should say, "Hey, I know you want to try this. Go ahead. Explore whatever kinds of opportunities and options you want. The world's your oyster."

Or maybe you'd do well to take the advice of author Barbara Sher, who in her book *Wishcraft* advises readers to throw caution to the wind and simply have fun brainstorming what they'd like to do. As if to give readers permission to do this, Sher suggests suspending all the rules of "reality," "possibility," "modesty"—"even the law of gravity" if it cramps your style.

- *Try stepping out of your "comfort zone."* As adults, we tend to be so serious about everything. We can get philosophically hidebound and queasy about the notion of stepping out of our comfort zone, even for a minute, to try new things. Yet sometimes our willingness to risk can help us "break out of the box" that is keeping us from exploring what we'd really like to do for a living. Don't worry about stumbling or making mistakes. You can't help but grow and gain perspective from such experiences. But it all starts with an honest inquiry of yourself, your aspirations and your abilities.

The "Going Through Focus" Technique

The process of asking yourself good questions is something I call the "going through focus" process. It's an extremely powerful technique for planning and managing your career.

If you're a photographer, you already know what I mean by the expression "going through focus." A photographer does this when he's trying to get a clear bead on the object in his lens. He shifts back and forth through focus before he actually locks in on a clear picture of what is in his field of vision.

In a similar way, asking yourself good questions is the way to begin focusing on what it is you want for yourself. As the pundit once put it, "All wisdom begins with a question."

If you know enough to ask yourself good questions about who you are, what you want for yourself, and how you can achieve what it is you dream about, you have what it takes to be successful.

Do you feel successful in your life right now? I would guess that even if you don't, you have more going for you than you think. So let's try something. Let's say, for the sake of argument, that you're not feeling good about your career. Maybe you've just lost your job or feel like it is in jeopardy. Or you feel stifled at work.

Answer the following questions and see if you don't feel differently about yourself and your situation after you've finished:

A Success Inventory

1. *What* do I feel good about in my life right now (e.g., family, relationship, kids, job)?
2. *What* have I done in the past six months (either on the job or in my personal life) that I'm proud of?
3. *Who* do I have in my life who cares about me?
4. *What* have I done for somebody else in the past month that made me feel good?
5. *What* do other people tell me makes me unique or special?

How do you feel? Do you have things going for you in your life? Of course you do! Maybe it's your family, your significant other, or friends who care about you. Maybe it's the realization that you have unique skills or abilities that are tapped rarely if at all. Maybe it's the fact that you did a great job on that big project at work, and even though your boss didn't acknowledge it (her problem, not yours), you still felt good about getting it done.

Training Your Brain to Find Pathways to Success

There is mounting evidence that suggests that the kinds of questions we ask ourselves each day can have a positive impact on our entire well-being: our emotions and our state of mind and the degree to which we feel empowered to go after what we want. Indeed, success coach Tony Robbins notes that the quality of questions we ask ourselves can determine the quality of our lives and is the key to both happiness and optimal human performance.

Take the time to ask yourself these questions: What can I do right now to position myself for better job and career opportunities in the future? What talents and skills do I have that I'd like to use in a next job?

In my opinion, asking yourself good questions can actually help your intellectual potential grow! A 1970 Stanford University study proved that most people operate on less than 5 percent of their mental capacity. If you can get in the habit of asking yourself good questions, you'll be far ahead of the 95 percent of the people in this world who go through life with blinders on or with self-imposed ideas of what's possible for them.

Throughout this book, I'm going to nudge you to ask yourself high-quality questions, questions designed to help you define and refine your professional goals and generate, explore, and play with job and career options.

You Are Already a Success

Did you know that the only way to be unsuccessful in this life is really to want something for yourself and *not* go for it—*not* take steps to find it, acquire it, earn it, or create it?

Acting on your career motivations is key to achieving them. It sounds simple, but millions of people fail to follow through.

Who succeeds in this world? People who first believe in themselves and who then are persistent, who possess enough presence of mind and psychological heartiness to keep forever on the heels of their dreams.

I'm not suggesting it's easy to persevere. And I'm not suggesting that stoicism is heroic or that you should always keep a stiff upper lip in the face of adversity. Indeed, at times I suggest quite the opposite (see Chapter 12).

If pursuing your dreams seems overwhelming (even paralyzing) at times or a little like an unrealistic fantasy, you may simply be trying to do things too quickly. It may be that you simply need to slow down a bit, take things one day at a time.

The Law of Cumulation

The most successful people put one foot in front of the other, day after day, aware of what's been called the law of cumulation*—lots of little steps that add up over time to significance and success.

Indeed, one of my cardinal rules of career planning is this:

> Managing your career is a process—not an event. It's something to do on a daily basis. If you take a one-day-at-time approach to managing your career, eventually all those little things you're doing for yourself each day will add up to some big changes—sometimes sooner than you think.

I first became aware of the law of cumulation back in high school. I was overwhelmed by the prospect of having to write a twenty-two-page paper for my sophomore history class. My teacher suggested I do just a little bit of work each day on this project. I followed her advice, and the paper almost wrote itself. It was done a week ahead of the deadline, and I got an "A" in the course.

*I am indebted to Drs. Roberta Kraus and John Anderson of the Center for Sports Psychology in Colorado Springs for first introducing me to this term.

Here are a few other folks who know something about the law of cumulation:

His Head Was in the Clouds

For years Gene Roddenberry was told by network TV executives that his concept for a science-fiction TV series about voyages to other planets was farfetched and would probably "never fly." But he refused to give up and persevered in his belief that American television viewers wanted high-quality science fiction on TV. Today, nearly thirty years after "Star Trek" premiered on television, the show has become part of our culture and lexicon. Who isn't familiar with the expression "Beam me up, Scotty!"? "Star Trek: The Next Generation" has been the most successful show in TV syndication today and people from youngsters to scientists (physicist Stephen Hawking is a fan) to seniors are fans of the show. Myself included.

He's Hardly Handicapped

Jim Abbott is a guy who doesn't know the meaning of the word *quit*. Nor does he let himself be hemmed in by societal expectations or by what some people might regard as his physical "limitations." In 1992 Jim became the first-ever one-armed pitcher to play in the major leagues. And in 1993, as a member of the New York Yankees, he became the first one-armed pitcher to pitch a no-hitter!

He Plays for Presidents and "Designing Women"

Ray Charles is another guy who didn't shrink from adversity early in his life, didn't forfeit his dreams because of difficult challenges or what others might have thought were physical limitations. As a singer and piano player Ray was blind and without parents at age 15, but that didn't stop him from forming a trio and going on the road. He's been wowing audiences—including presidents and kings—with his gentle blend of jazz and blues ever since.

She Earned Her Place in the Daytime Limelight

Even before she became the phenomenal talk-show sensation she is today, Sally Jessy Raphael knew she had a talent for talking to people and for asking compelling questions of guests—the kinds of questions that make her show riveting. Even though, by her own reckoning, she's been fired no fewer than eighteen times from radio jobs on her way to the top of the talk-show pack, she kept going and going and going, outlasting even the Energizer Bunny!

You may not aspire to produce a TV series, pitch in the major leagues, start your own band, or have your own radio or television talk show. That doesn't matter. I want to affirm you in whatever it is you want to do—because the only thing that counts is how *you* define success.

A Blessing in Disguise?

We're living in turbulent economic times. Downsizings and corporate restructurings continue to result in the layoff of thousands of people.

Yet I believe that the diminished job security in today's economy may be a blessing in disguise—at least for some people. Here's why.

While being laid off or outplaced from a job can be scary, it also creates new opportunities for people. The Chinese symbol for *crisis*, after all, also contains within it the symbol for *opportunity*.

Many times people I have worked with in job and career transition later come back to me with comments like:

> I never would have asked to be laid off from my job, but in some ways it has been an opportunity of growth for me. I hated what I was doing. In the last few months, I've had a chance to rethink my values and what's really important to me. I've had a chance to watch my son grow and to be there for my daughter as she went through a painful operation. I've recast my definition of success. I'm not willing to be a slave to somebody else at this point in my life. What I want is to strike a better balance in my life and create something of my own.

So how do *you* want to define success?

While, in fact, many jobs in corporate America are going away and may never return, other kinds of opportunities are emerging. Consider, for example, contract employment, interim management and executive jobs, telecommuting opportunities, work-from-home options, consultative possibilities, and start-up ventures. These are just a few of the new and emerging ways of work in today's economy. In many cases, they are affording people greater flexibility and more options than they enjoyed in previous jobs.

A Public Relations Entrepreneur

"Jason" is a successful and happy forty-one-year-old consultant who has been an independent contractor for the past ten years. In growing his business, Jason has used not only his skills in training and marketing but his love of public relations and writing to help him position his company in the small business marketplace. Indeed, these things have created very powerful and positive "synergy" for him in his business.

"I've had a great time being in business for myself," he says. "Launching this business has enabled me to use a wide range of my talents in ways I was never able to do before."

Prior to hanging out a shingle as an independent human resources consultant, Jason worked in training and development for one of America's largest companies. While he acknowledges that working for a large corporation taught him a great deal about business, the bureaucracy, the politics, and the protocol of the place drove him nuts:

> When I worked in this company, I was acknowledged as having many talents in the areas of writing, public relations, and the stand-up delivery of training programs and other things. But the rigid system of job descriptions and salary grades kept me from being able to do most of these things for most of the time I was with the company. The company was extremely level-conscious, and as a mid-level manager I didn't have much latitude or autonomy to do anything. It was so frustrating, because more than anything else the company seemed to want to corral me in a box.

Jason says that as a small-business owner and operator, he doesn't yet have the kind of financial security he wants but he's making an excellent living and loves the latitude and autonomy, the "psyche pay," of being his own boss: "I wouldn't trade what I'm doing for anything. I doubt that I will ever want to work for anyone else again, because, in the last analysis, I really don't enjoy trying to please somebody else as much as I do myself."

A Franchise Owner

"Jim" is someone else who has left the world of large organizations to become his own boss—in his case, to become a franchise owner.

After a long and largely satisfying job in the military, Jim decided a few years ago to start a printing business with his wife and another business partner.

"One spring afternoon I was at the Pentagon, and I walked outside and thought, 'I'm going to get out of this.' I wasn't mad or anything. But I thought, 'I'm just going to do something different.'"

In the military, Jim had a great deal of exposure to the printing industry, so it was natural that he should explore getting into the printing business. After doing some research, he, his wife, and a business partner bought a PIP Printing franchise.

Today Jim and his partner own four separate PIP Printing franchises in Northern Virginia. In 1993 their business took in just under $2 million.

In some ways, running a business is not unlike what he did in the military, Jim says. He uses his knowledge of "warfare" when it comes to marketing his business's products and services, for example. "In a way, business is like a war. It's a battle, and the more information you have on what your competition's doing or what your clients want, the better," Jim says.

He also uses his leadership and managerial skills daily to keep the business operating and to manage and motivate his "troops."

Jim is quick to say that running a business isn't for everybody, but it's brought him tremendous satisfaction.

> A lot of the time I look at it like a game. You like to win. You don't always win. Every once in a while you get knocked down, but you pick yourself back up again. There's a lot of fun in that, and hey, let's see if we can score another point today. And I like people. It is a lot of fun to work with people.

Jim's advice to anyone who's considering starting a business is this: "If you're happy working eight hours a day, stay where you are because you've got to be willing to work hard and at odd hours." He adds, "I've seen some guys who come out of big corporations—*Fortune* 500 corporations—and try to start their own business. A lot of them fail miserably because they weren't willing to put the time in initially. They were used to huge support staffs and had huge budgets that they weren't really held accountable for."

A Peripatetic Actor

"Frank" makes his living starring in television commercials, doing radio and TV voiceovers, and performing with an acting troupe that tours the country. He's also appeared in more than twenty movies and TV shows, including such hits as *Dead Poets Society*, *The Tin Men*, *DC Cab*, and "America's Most Wanted."

How did Frank get into acting? He always had an interest in it, but the idea of doing it full-time didn't hit him until he was an adult. One day, sitting in a movie theatre watching the film *That's Entertainment*, Frank decided he wanted to see his own face up on the silver screen. It was then that he decided to quit his job as a clerk-typist for the federal government. "I came to the conclusion that a benevolent God couldn't possibly mean for me to sit at that blasted desk for the rest of my life! My life felt meaningless," he says.

Nowadays, Frank divides his time between acting gigs, tryouts for new parts, and preparing himself for what he hopes will soon be his first talking role in a major Hollywood movie.

Although he doesn't make much money as an actor, Frank says he wouldn't give up acting for anything. At the same time, however, he acknowledges that his definition of success is a far cry from that of many other people:

> You give up what I think society terms as "stability" and what it may even term "success." I have not given up the dream of owning my own home one day. That is a solid goal that I have. But I've pretty much given up the luxury of buying a new car every two years, of having a lot of money in the bank, the luxury of being able to travel, even going out to dinner at will.

The New "Success"—From Credenzas to a Balanced Life

Mary Crannell, a small-business owner and the sole employee of her own human resources consulting business, believes that Jason, Jim, and Frank are typical of a growing number of people in society today. They have tasted financial and professional success or have known the feeling of job security, yet they have forsaken the standard criteria of success to do something different and more meaningful with their lives.

Each, she says, is looking for something more from his work than simply a paycheck—be it autonomy or the chance to do something different or to be responsible for creating his own job security.

"In the 1980s, the mentality was 'whoever dies with the most toys wins.' That's what determined success," she says. "And if you worked in corporate America and were above a certain level, you got two credenzas in your office, as well as an oak desk, a closed door, and a window. That was how corporations defined success."

Today, Crannell believes the tide has turned: "In the 1990s, we're seeing a real shift in how people define success. As big-time corporate America continues to downsize, reorganize, and restructure itself, more and more people are asking themselves, 'What do I want?' And it's no longer just a monetary thing. People are looking for flexibility, the ability to balance their lives, the opportunity to enjoy a higher quality of life. Even spirituality is coming back, and the desire to make a difference. Those are things we haven't seen since the 1960s."

Zeroing in on *Your* Definition of Success

For you, success may mean owning a business, feeding the homeless, or driving a Lexus. Whatever it means, define it, know you deserve it, and go after it. Today.

Take out a tablet of paper and answer the questions that follow. Don't hurry through this exercise. Be thoughtful and reflective about what you want. After all, we are looking to identify the things that are of greatest value to you in a job or career.

How Do You Define Success?

1. What do you have to have in a job to feel successful? Check as many of the following as you want.
   - ___ Good salary
   - ___ Good benefits
   - ___ Opportunity for advancement
   - ___ Recognition for my work
   - ___ Latitude/autonomy
   - ___ Opportunity to create
   - ___ Opportunity to manage/develop other people
   - ___ Opportunity to learn
   - ___ Opportunity to be part of a team
   - ___ Flexible hours
   - ___ Chance to help other people
   - ___ Opportunity to provide good customer service
   - ___ Brisk pace
   - ___ Relaxed environment
   - ___ Stability in the position
   - ___ Independence

- Intellectual challenge
- Enlightened management
- Responsibility
- Power
- Opportunity to create original work
- Opportunity to do something novel or unique
- Opportunity to do something good for society
- Opportunity to create wealth
- Influence others
- Team building
- Nice environment
- Other: (specify)

2. Now rank the ten most important things from this list.
3. Now rank the five most important things from the list of ten items.
4. How many of those things do you have right now?
5. Write down, in two or three paragraphs, your personal definition of success.
6. What do you feel good about in your job/career right now? Include scope of responsibilities you currently have, recent projects you are proud of, awards and other kinds of recognition you have received.
7. What would you like to do if you were to leave your company? Be specific.
8. How can you begin positioning yourself for your next job, be it with your current employer or another employer?
9. Again, write out your personal definition of success. This time use a full page, and use strong action verbs to describe the kinds of things you want to be doing.

A Sleuth in Pursuit of Yourself

Give yourself sufficient time to do the preceding exercise. If it helps, talk out your answers onto a tape recorder, or discuss them with a close friend before writing them down.

This exercise is not idle navel gazing. It's healthy reflection intended to help you define what you want from your job and career. I call it "being a sleuth in pursuit of yourself." As I often tell people in workshops, "Half the battle in reaching goals is deciding where you want to go."

There's another axiom that comes into play here as well: "The better you know yourself, the more likely you are to find what you're looking for." After all, knowledge is power. And self-knowledge is empowering.

As you continue through this book, keep the definition of success you came up with in this chapter close at hand. Indeed, think of this definition of success as a kind of professional amulet you're going to wear around your neck for good luck as you embark on your job hunt or career transition.

Defining personal and professional success is one of the critical underpinnings of effective career management. But your definition of success doesn't have to be cast in concrete. Quite the opposite. You may find that your idea of success evolves over time as you identify your skills, explore your options, talk with people, and discover what may be a new professional passion!

HABIT #3

Learn How to Transfer Your Skills and Leverage Your Experience

> Be it chess, market forces, basket weaving, or engineering—know one system in its depth. Go beyond the rules of thumb until you can express in your own words its ins and outs. Go to the point where you seldom find a book or article that tells you anything new about your chosen field. Go to the point where you can accurately surmise that which you have not been told.
>
> —John Cowan
> *Small Decencies: Reflections and Meditations on Being Human at Work*

In his book, *The Fifth Discipline,* Peter Senge talks about the parable of the "boiled frog." If you were to put a frog into a pot of boiling water, the story goes, it would immediately try to leap to safety. However, if you were to increase the water temperature ever so slightly over time, the frog would not leap to safety, but be poached alive in the steadily increasing warmth of the water.

Why would this happen?

Because the changes taking place in the water temperature would be so gradual they would be indiscernible to the frog, who would lack the foresight to leap out of the pot and out of harm's way.

In today's business world too many people act like this poached frog. They fail to take stock of the microchanges taking place in the economy and workplace around them on a daily basis. Moreover, they fail to keep up with the latest developments in their industry or business—and with the skills required to do their job.

In essence, like that frog, they fail to respond appropriately to the changes in their environment. Thus, they run the risk of having very unfortunate things happen to them at work.

What can you do to avoid becoming a poached frog on the job? In a word, become more "response-able." Develop the capacity to respond in multiple and flexible ways to the changing business and workplace climate around you.

In this economy, developing "response-ability" is not only critical to career success and stability, it's also the shortest route to finding personal happiness and professional fulfillment. For the more "response-able" you are, the more opportunities and options you will have to choose from. In fact, the more likely you are to have opportunities coming and looking for you!

The way to become "response-able" is to become conversant with your skills and how they can be used not only in your current job but potentially in other positions and careers as well. Your future career success also depends on keeping your skills, like an athlete's muscles, toned and in fighting trim.

Many economists and educators have observed that the education and skills of the American workforce are the only things that can serve as competitive weapons in the twenty-first century, when countries will be pitted against one another for a piece of the economic pie.

If we personalize that forecast a bit and speak not of the world economy but of you in particular, it's fair to say that your education and skills will be your most effective competitive weapon in the battle for the best jobs.

Look at today's information-based economy. The best wages today go to people who are "knowledge workers"—people with top-tier skills and expertise in areas such as science, engineering, finance, management, technology, and economics. That trend will continue and intensify in the next century.

As noted economist Lester Thurow observes in his book *Head to Head*, "Consider what are commonly believed to be the seven key industries of the next few decades—microelectronics, biotechnology, the new materials industries, civilian aviation, telecommunications, robots plus machine tools, and computers plus software. All are brainpower industries."[1]

1. Lester Thurow, *Head to Head: The Coming Economic Battle Among Japan, Europe, and America* (New York: Warner Books, 1993), p. 45.

Years ago, only doctors and engineers had to be concerned with keeping their skills "cutting-edge." Today, however, everybody needs to be concerned about professional obsolescence. Even hairdressers and driving school instructors need to keep up with regular developments in their fields. Knowledge in every field is expanding so rapidly that if you don't make an effort to keep up, your skills and expertise can become stale and outmoded almost overnight. As business consultant Pat Lynch puts it, "It's not what you know you don't know that can hurt you in business today, it's what you don't know you don't know that will!"

This is particularly true in fields related to science and mathematics, fields that, according to most studies, hold the most promise of employment in the years ahead. But it's also true in the world of business.

Since the early 1990s, a rather lengthy list of corporate CEOs has been ousted as their companies have undergone downsizing and restructuring. Why has this occurred?

A January 18, 1993, article in *The New York Times* entitled "Turning Out the Insiders" chronicled the fates of eight of these CEOs. It suggested that dozens of factors in today's business environment, including global competition, shifting consumer tastes, and the accelerating rate of technological change in the workplace, were challenges to which these old-line business executives were not able to respond with sufficient speed and agility.[2] In the final analysis, these men lacked what I refer to as the "professional gauge" necessary to do their jobs. In other words, they lacked certain critical skills and experience in sufficient measure and proportion to be effective in their positions.

You don't want to suffer the fate of these CEOs. You don't want to be perceived as professionally obsolete or as lacking sufficient "professional gauge" to do your job. To avoid this, become a keen student of the business environment around you.

Nine Trends to Keep in Mind if You Want to Remain a "State-of-the-Art" Professional

1. *Work and learning will be more closely integrated than they have been in the past.* We are already entering the age of the "learning organization," which, as David Garvin describes it in the *Harvard Business Review*, is an organization skilled at five discrete activities: problem solving, experimenting with new approaches, learning from past experiences, learning

---

2. "Turning Out the Insiders," *The New York Times*, January 18, 1993, p. D1.

from the best practices of others, and transferring knowledge quickly and efficiently throughout the organization.[3]

The integration of work and learning is being driven by the continually expanding role of technology in the workplace, the push in all organizations to move close to their customers, and the business imperative to operate more efficiently. In this context, the traditional manager (e.g., somebody who delegates work to others) is being replaced by "stand-alone" professionals (people who frequently work alone except for a computer) and by self-directed teams empowered to make decisions and solve problems closer to the point of origin. As a 1993 survey by the *Employment Management Association* put it: "Bureaucratic layers of form approvers, information passers, and other intermediaries are being wiped off the organization charts, as greater control . . . is given to those with hands-on involvement."[4]

To contribute and compete effectively as a professional in this kind of environment, you will need to possess hands-on or "shirt-sleeve" skills (e.g., computer literacy); personal and intellectual self-confidence; an ability to learn, adapt, absorb, and apply new information quickly and readily to your work; and an appreciation for the give-and-take of group decision making, problem solving, and brainstorming.

2. *In the learning organization, keeping your functional, professional, and technical skills up-to-date will be critical to your professional effectiveness.* You will need to audit the status of your skills and experience on an ongoing basis to ensure that your hands-on skills remain state-of-the-art. This will be a significant challenge in a workplace of accelerating change and in which the demands of work will easily crowd out developmental opportunities and professional self-reflection if you don't commit yourself to it.

3. *There will be fewer opportunities for traditional upward mobility.* Instead of thinking that the only definition of career success is to move continually upward on a professional ladder in an organization, you'll want to consider options or ways to develop yourself that might involve creating your own job description, rotating into a lateral position to broaden your experience, or even taking a short-term pay cut if it goes with a professional experience that you need to get as part of your strategic career plan.

3. David Garvin, "Building a Learning Organization," *Harvard Business Review*, July–August 1993, p. 164.
4. "EMA 1993 Employment Market Survey," Employment Management Association, Raleigh, N.C., pp. 2–6.

4. *To be successful, you'll need to be more than a trained technician or "parochial professional" immersed in the details of your discipline.* You will need to develop a global perspective about your work and its interrelationship with that of others in your organization, and "organizational competencies" to help you function successfully within the workplace. Jane Shore, an organizational career development consultant and coauthor of *Organizational Career Development,* believes that there are several organizational "core competencies" that any professional needs to develop:

> As much as you need to be technically or professionally competent in your area of expertise . . . you also need to know how to work well in groups, be able to communicate effectively with others, learn quickly, adapt to change, lead others, take risks, build relationships across levels and functions, and sustain a focus on quality and on the "customer" in your organization. . . . These kinds of things will be important even for technical people to do.

Developing such competencies will be important, because while technology will enable some people to work more effectively as individual contributors, most people will still work in the context of a team environment.

5. *Given the continued decline of organizational hierarchies and the increased role of information technology at work, you will have less direct supervision than in the past but also be held more closely accountable for the work you do.* You may not necessarily have much day-to-day contact with your boss or even be located in the same city, yet you will be rigorously monitored and evaluated in terms of the "value-added" contribution you make to your organization's bottom line. This will be true not just for people in sales and marketing but for those in virtually all other departments, from operations and customer service to training, accounting, and public relations. To operate effectively in this kind of environment you will need to shed the docility that was so often a part of the workplace in corporate America and to become an effective self-starter, able to operate as a team player one moment and as an individual contributor the next.

I have coached a lot of people who have moved out of jobs in *Fortune* 500 companies and have gone to work for start-up ventures or for small or mid-size companies requiring this kind of professional agility. What they find is that they can't hide from either the risks or the responsibilities of hands-on management, be it of themselves, their employees, or their bottom line.

As one client of mine put it: "In my old job there wasn't that much individual accountability. Everything got lost in the bureaucracy. Here, it's a lot easier to see the ground under your feet because it's right there just inches away from you!"

6. *As part of your ongoing professional development, expect to change jobs every two to four years and employers every three to five years.* Why? Because you'll need to enhance your professional portfolio of skills and experience every way you can—and chances are no single employer will give you the breadth of experience that you can collect on your own if you make both tactical and strategic career moves. As recruiter John Lucht, author of *Rites of Passage at $100,000+*, has noted, the savviest professionals in any industry are those who know not only how to do a good job in their current job but how to do a good job of getting another job.

7. *There will be a continuing opportunity to create new paradigms of work, built around new models of leadership, group interaction, product and process quality, and advancing workplace technology.* Corporations and organizations will continue to struggle with and to define the need for new styles of leadership as they seek ways to foster greater employee commitment and productivity. Total Quality Management (TQM) and business process reengineering (BPR) are but two of the latest models of organizational renewal that businesses and organizations are seeking to implement in the workplace in order to increase productivity and profitability, as well as organizational vitality. They are, in many ways, rapidly redefining and redesigning the nature of jobs as organizations try to figure out how best to manage and motivate people in the post-downsizing era.

At the same time, the accelerating pace of technological change, particularly miniaturization, will continue to transform what we define as work, especially for knowledge workers and highly skilled professionals. Already, technology is speeding the arrival of things such as "the office in a box," a briefcase equipped with cellular phone, fax, color LCD, printers, and keyboards.[5] It's also ushering in the era of professional "lone eagles" (see Chapter 7).

8. *To be successful in the next century, you will need to think of organizational change not as a disruption to your work but as the focus of your work.*

5. "Seven Trends That Will Change Your Future Worklife," *Personnel News*, May 1993.

You will need to develop psychological heartiness to deal effectively with the stress of organizational change. This will be important whether you're in the position of managing other people, working as part of a team, or functioning as an individual contributor.

Those who will make the most successful career transitions will be those who are flexible, team-oriented, energized by change, and tolerant of ambiguity and who have relatively low control needs. At the same time, people who have a big need for clarity, control, and certainty may be frustrated by the corporate and organizational workplace of the future.[6]

9. *Finally, as bosses, mentors, and teammates come and go, you'll need to develop alliances with a broad range of people in your organization and find unique ways to sell yourself.* In his book *Blow Your Own Horn: How to Get Noticed and Get Ahead,* Jeffrey Davidson says those who get ahead in their professional lives are natural born marketers. Today, you need to be mindful of this. Recognize that your compatibility with other people and the degree to which you promote and position yourself effectively are just as important to your career success as your professional competence.

Using Your Twenty-First-Century Skills to Create Job Pathways

If you become organizationally astute and commit yourself to keeping your skills up-to-date, they can provide you with multiple pathways to other jobs and careers throughout your working life. Many skills are quite portable and can be applied in virtually any organization or industry. Skills such as writing, public speaking, financial and human resources management, salesmanship, computer competency, and delivering training programs are especially valuable.

Besides your skills, get acquainted with your talents—the often unused, undervalued, or even undiscovered gifts that you possess. Perhaps you are a natural writer, trainer, or presenter, so much so that you have written articles for publications outside your company or been asked to give major presentations for your boss, who is scared to death of public speaking. Pay attention to ways you might develop and use these talents in your current job or in a new and different job. Talents, like skills, are always in demand, and you may not be getting as much professional mileage out of them as you could.

6. "EMA 1993 Employment Market Survey," Employment Management Association, Raleigh, N.C., pp. 2–6.

Many of us overlook the gifts that make us unique. I've worked with many people who never thought their talents could be readily or practically applied in the workplace.

"Jeff" is a bright and highly talented technical writer and graphic artist who for years had trouble "owning" the natural artistic and linguistic talents he possessed. Jeff excelled in English and graphic arts from an early age, but his parents didn't affirm these abilities in him when he was a child. Consequently, he struggled for years to get his career on track and to feel good about the talents that were languishing inside him. "I never really valued my talents because my parents never really did," he notes. "I had some significant self-esteem issues that kept me from acknowledging my abilities and that kept me from appreciating the fact that I have talents people need—and that employers are willing to pay for."

Nowadays, Jeff is a happily employed computer-graphics designer and technical writer who has effectively blended a love of English with an aptitude for computers. He conceives, formats, and produces a wide range of sales and marketing materials, including sales proposals, training manuals, technical guidebooks, and brochures. His colleagues in the office love his work because he brings a combination of skills to the workplace that nobody else in his office has. His talents have made him indispensable.

Then, there's "Mort," a forty-nine-year-old government worker who for years has worked in the field of defense intelligence. For some time, I have worked with Mort to help him find a more satisfying line of work.

One day, as we sat in my office talking, he told me about one of his favorite hobbies—cartooning. The more I listened to Mort and watched the light dance in his eyes, the more I suspected that cartooning was where Mort's passion really lay and where he should be building a career. But he had never thought of turning his talent for drawing into something that could make him a living.

"Why don't you put together a portfolio of your work and come back to see me in two weeks?" I said.

Mort did what I asked. Two weeks later he showed up at the office, proudly bearing a portfolio of drawings, some of which he'd drawn more than twenty years ago. As I leafed through the pages, examining the characters in each of his drawings, I let out a hoot: "These are great, Mort!" Afterward I showed them to my colleagues in the office, who by their chuckles gave Mort's work a similar sign of approval.

Over a period of months, Mort began exploring the possibility of making a long-time hobby of his into a full-time living. He has since added new drawings to his portfolio and met with several prominent editorial cartoonists in the Washington, D.C., area to discuss the possibilities of getting syndicated. He is excited by what he hears from the people he is meeting with and has landed a part-time assignment to provide illustrations for a professional newsletter.

The dilemma that Jeff and Mort have had to deal with is not uncommon. Often, people with artistic, musical, dramatic, or other creative talents are not affirmed in the practice of those things as a career—and they often need encouragement to do so.

You yourself may have some other kind of ability or talent that was squelched in you. If you enjoy using that ability, I encourage you to find ways to incorporate it into your work.

Leveraging Your Experience Into Other Fields

You may not realize this, but people make moves into new jobs and careers all the time. They leverage the experience gained in one field or profession and use it as a "pivot point" into something else. While sometimes you need special education and training to switch gears, it isn't always a requirement.

A prominent radio talk-show host I know began her radio career as a volunteer and eventually parlayed that volunteer job into a paid position of considerable prominence in her community. Today, her radio show is literally the "talk of the town" in her community. It regularly features a parade of celebrities, politicians, authors, and other notables with whom she has engaging conversations.

Then there's the case of "Susan." Susan is a former mortgage banker who a few years ago decided to switch gears and move into another career entirely. A true career seeker, she has worked on Capitol Hill, in a law office, in teaching positions, and in business. Today she is in the midst of becoming an Episcopal priest, confident that the broad portfolio of experience she acquired while working in business, finance, and the law will be invaluable to her in the ministry.

"Certainly I will use my degree in psychology and my writing skills," she says. "I have worked in law and politics, so I can't help but think that that will give me a sense of how to deal with 'political' situations that may arise."

Susan believes her experience in business and finance will be especially helpful when she administers a parish and needs to approach people for money—something she says a lot of clergy have a tough time doing. Finally, she notes, having taught religion to kids "will enhance any kind of future liturgy, music, and teaching that I do down the road.

"Nothing I have done has been for naught. It has all been a piece of a huge puzzle that is being put together. And whether or not I could have done things differently, I didn't. But I have this breadth of experience that makes me capable, interesting, and equipped."

There are, of course, many famous people who have made successful career transitions.

- Thirty years of acting experience provided Jane Alexander with an ideal background to become chair of the National Endowment for the Arts.
- Ronald Reagan used his acting talents in no small measure to transition out of acting into politics.
- Ernest Hemingway used the skills he learned as a journalist to develop the spare signature style of his many books.
- Comedian John Cleese has created a business empire for himself by leveraging his Monty Python comedic skills into the somewhat prosaic world of corporate training films.
- Author Joseph Wambaugh, one-time cop with the Los Angeles police department, has quite literally made a financial killing writing books, such as *The Killing Fields,* which draw upon his vast professional background.

For every famous person out there who has made a career transition, there are thousands if not hundreds of thousands of others, not well-known, who have done the very same thing.

Creating a Synergy of Skills, Talents, and Experience

Your background—consisting of your skills, your talents, and what I like to refer as your "compelling personal experience" in a job—has broader applicability than you might think. (See Figure 3-1.) Sure, if you're a landscape architect and you want to become a brain surgeon you have a longer road to take than most. But in many cases, the synergy of your skills, talents, and experience, creatively mixed together, can provide you with an ideal platform for moving into new fields or professions.

If you start to think of your professional assets in this way—as a "suitcase" or portfolio of skills—you will begin to get a sense of the amount of professional "horsepower" you can bring to other jobs and the ways in which your unique background and experience can differentiate you from other job-seekers.

Figure 3-1. Overlapping skills, talents, and experience.

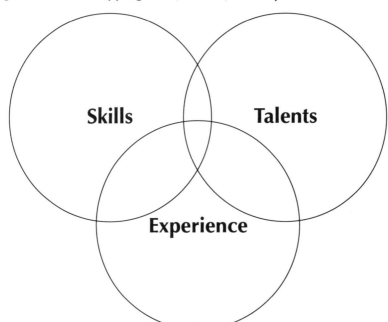

Indeed, thinking of yourself as having a portfolio of skills, skills that can be leveraged in multiple ways in the marketplace, enables you to entertain a wide variety of options. It can open up the door to any number of jobs and careers that are derivative of one another.

Defining Your Portfolio of Skills, Talents, and Experience

So, what's in your professional "suitcase" of skills and talents? What compelling personal or professional experience do you possess that could provide you with pivot points into other jobs and careers?

Using the "Going Through Focus" Technique I am going to ask you to answer some questions, from which we will determine your core skills and abilities. In doing this exercise, you'll also generate examples of your skills and abilities in action in past jobs and careers. (See Figure 3-2.)

I like to think of these things as "moments of professional glory" on the job—things you did and enjoyed but for which you may not have been rewarded or recognized by your boss or employer at the time.

Figure 3-2. Using the "Going Through Focus" Technique to chronicle your accomplishments at work.

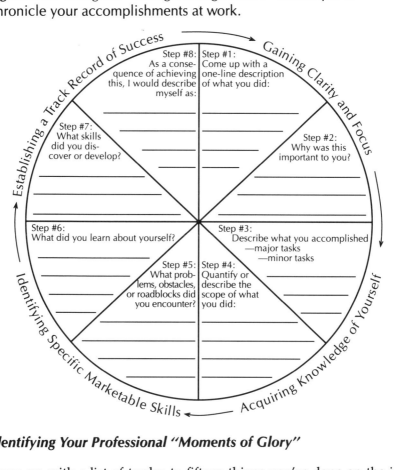

Identifying Your Professional "Moments of Glory"

Come up with a list of twelve to fifteen things you've done on the job (both in your current position and in past jobs) that brought you satisfaction and which you are proud of.

Remember, a "moment of professional glory" is something you've done that you are proud of, that showcases one or more of your skills "in action," and for which you may or may not have been recognized and rewarded by your boss at the time you did it.

For instance, did you:

- Train people in the use of a new computer software package?
- Create a new automated accounting system for your department?
- Increase operating efficiency in your corporate division?

- Implement a new procedure that reduced costs?
- Write an article for a trade publication?
- Create a way to do a job more efficiently but with fewer people?
- Manage and coordinate a special project that involved you in team-leading a group of other professionals?
- Increase sales?
- Develop a new product or service?
- Start a new department and/or hire staff?
- Create publicity or visibility for your organization?
- Give product or service demonstrations to customers?
- Manage an office move?

Cataloguing Your Moments of Glory

There is virtually an endless variety of categories under which you might organize your moments of personal and professional glory. For purposes of getting you thinking about what you've done in past jobs, you may want to think in terms of things you've done in the following areas:

- Sales and marketing
- Data processing
- Technical writing
- Quality management
- Public relations
- Financial management
- Administration
- Management
- Writing/editing
- Sales/marketing support
- Strategic planning
- Fund raising
- Customer relations
- Research and development
- Training and development
- Customer service
- Project management
- Leadership
- Events planning/coordination
- Software development
- Accounting
- Supervision
- Desk-top publishing
- Budget planning/forecasting
- Investment/asset management
- Product/service development
- Budget analysis and control
- Donor/membership development

In chronicling each item, be as specific as possible. First, come up with a one-line description or "headline" that describes what you did. For example, perhaps you successfully expanded the customer service department of your organization or reduced departmental costs over a six-month period.

Next, describe why this accomplishment is personally significant or special to you.

Third, describe what you actually achieved. What was the task you set out to accomplish? What were all the little sub-tasks you did that led up to it becoming a reality?

For instance, if you were responsible for managing a big system upgrade of your company's computer equipment, you undertook many specific activities to accomplish this. You might have been responsible for assembling a team of people in your office to help implement the upgrade. You may have solicited bids from prospective vendors, developed the "specs" for a technical bid that was distributed to vendors, and so forth. In answering this question, highlight the specific subtasks you undertook.

Next, try to quantify or qualify each accomplishment. Then describe the difficulties (if any) that you encountered along the way.

Your particular skills should pop out at you by the end of this exercise. You should also be able to come up with some good labels that accurately describe the kind of person you are at work. For instance, the moments of glory you chronicle may reveal that you're persistent, politically savvy, or detail-oriented.

This is probably the single hardest exercise you will do in this book. It may, in fact, seem arduous and unnecessary. Believe me, for purposes of setting goals, writing a strong résumé, and talking with people about what you want to do professionally, it's critical. Completing this exercise, in fact, lays the groundwork for crafting your résumé and for the networking activities we talk about in later chapters.

Acknowledging Your Strengths

A lot of times when people are asked to talk about things they've done at work that made a difference—that contributed to productivity, to profitability, to helping people, or to improving efficiency—they tend to go blank. "I've never done anything special; I've just always done my job," I often hear people say.

That's not true. You undoubtedly contributed more to your organization than you realize. It may be, however, that until now nobody (including you) stopped to think about what you contributed. I'm giving you permission to do that.

Become conversant with your accomplishments! As John Cowan, a priest, sailor, consultant, and philosopher, noted in his nifty little book, *Small Decencies: Reflections and Meditations on Being Human at Work*, "Our accomplishments are not too simple, mundane, and ordinary to merit a moment of glory. We deserve to have our fellow workers sing our song."

Chronicling Your Moments of Professional Glory

1. Come up with a list of twelve to fifteen things that you're proud of having accomplished at work.
2. What makes each of these accomplishments so special to you?
3. In each case, what did you actually achieve? Why was this important to your organization?
   - My goal was to. . . .
   - To accomplish this, I did the following things. . . .

4. If you can, quantify the benefits that came from your accomplishment (e.g., "Increased sales by 20 percent in a three-year period"). If you can't, can you describe the scope of what you did (e.g., "Delivered training programs to more than two hundred company managers in ten states over a six-month period")?
5. What kinds of challenges or obstacles did you face (e.g., problems relating to people, office politics, budget, managing a "process," or meeting critical deadlines)?
6. What did you learn about yourself from your task?
7. What *specific* skills did you demonstrate "in action" as you worked toward your achievement?
8. Finally, come up with some good adjectives or phrases (e.g., goal-oriented, team player, results-oriented, detail-oriented, politically astute) to describe the kind of person you proved yourself to be by your accomplishment.

Once you take time to become conversant with your accomplishments at work, as well as the skills you used to achieve them, you will have done a lot of the mental spadework necessary to embark on a job search, begin a career transition to another field, or simply explore your professional options in more depth.

You will generate a lot of material by completing this "scratchpad" exercise in a diligent and thorough way, but hang on to your notes.

You'll want to refer to them later, especially when we talk about résumés in Chapter 6.

You've worked hard, so before you go on to Chapter 4, take a break. Go to the gym, take yourself out to lunch, or just kick back and be a couch potato for once. You've earned it!

HABIT #4

Develop a Vision of the Future and an Action Plan to Get You There

> The great end of life is not knowledge but action.
> —Thomas Huxley

Have you tried at times to set career goals for yourself, only to fall back into old patterns of inaction, dissatisfaction, and passivity after a few days or weeks?

Lots of people have trouble actualizing their dreams. It isn't because their dreams aren't worthwhile or achievable. And it isn't because people don't try or because they lack the discipline or drive to do what they want to do.

There are four main reasons we fail to achieve our dreams.

1. Many people fail to plan, so in effect they plan to fail. As my colleague Bob Worley is fond of saying, "Most people put more time into planning a vacation than they do into planning a career!"

2. Other people get diverted and distracted from their primary goals and desires by a million little things (most administrative and logistical) that demand their attention and sap their energy. In Chapter 1 I referred to this as the phenomenon of becoming "distracted by Elvis."

3. Still others tend to get caught up in a cycle of activities and busyness that revolves around other people and their lives and needs. While taking care of others can be laudable and is in some cases necessary (e.g., a couple may elect to do "tag-team" parenting, with each parent

spending time away from work in order to care for a child), it's not wise for anyone to put aside *indefinitely* their career goals for other things.

Many people, women particularly, need to pay attention to their tendency to defer their interests, needs, or desires to those of others. Because women so often are reared to be caregivers, they frequently disregard their own interests, goals, and dreams and focus instead on the wishes of others, living vicariously through children, siblings, or husbands.

"Betsy," for instance, is a fifty-one-year-old mother of two who spent thirteen years teaching before getting married. Although she loved raising kids, she wishes today that she had returned to the workforce earlier than she did.

> I think a career is every bit as important to a woman as to a man. I wish I had spent more time earlier in my life developing my career. But when I was growing up I was still on the very traditional track of getting married and having children and putting my own career aside to raise children and take care of my husband. Today, if I had it to do over again, I would either go to law school or to medical school. Moreover, I would have gone back to school earlier, and I would have been more insistent on meeting that need for myself.

It isn't just women who often put the concerns and needs of others before themselves. Other people do it as well—at times for very unhealthy and even dysfunctional reasons. Children of alcoholics (COAs) and other people who tend to be "co-dependent" in their relationships fall into this category. They frequently put their lives on hold while they worry about somebody else's welfare. Indeed, COAs often speak of the feeling of "living someone else's life" rather than their own.

I'm living proof of this fact. As the child of an alcoholic, it was all too easy for me in years past to get hooked into taking care of other people (parents, employers, significant others), all the while neglecting my own interests, needs, and desires.

4. Some people try to do too much too fast. As a result, they become overwhelmed by the enormity of what they set out to do for themselves, become discouraged, and quit before they've even gotten started.

Remember, however, that an Olympic runner doesn't achieve the cardiovascular capacity she needs to run the distance in just a few days.

Nor does a jazz pianist or clarinetist pick up his instrument one day and start headlining at the Rainbow Room the next.

Creating a Vision for the Future

It takes *p*lanning, *p*reparation, and *p*atience and at least a little time to achieve most goals and dreams. There are three aspects to creating a vision for the future and an action plan for getting there:

    1. You must pursue your goals and dreams with a great deal of *focus*. This means developing clear and highly specific career goals and objectives for yourself.

    2. You must believe in the *goodness* and *attainability* of your goals. This means becoming accountable to yourself for results. It means acknowledging what you really want and then going after it with all the energy and vigor you can muster.

    3. You must strive towards reaching your goals and dreams *one day at a time*. To do this effectively, you need to pursue your goals methodically as part of a career action plan.

Focusing on What You Want

Remember the law of cumulation? I mentioned it back in Chapter 2 when I was talking about how successful people become successful. They pursue their goals by becoming focused and by pursuing their objectives on a dogged and ongoing basis. They don't expect to make the earth move with just a single step, yet they know that any journey begins that way. They pursue their goals with consistency, having faith that if they take lots of little steps their efforts will add up in time to success.

    This is what comedian Jay Leno did to become a successful comic and to position himself as Johnny Carson's successor on *The Tonight Show*. As writer Bill Carter notes in his book *The Late Shift: Letterman, Leno, and the Network Battle for the Night:*

> For Leno a career in show business was not something you dreamed about, it was something you worked on—like a car. *The Tonight Show* was a mecca because it was where comic reputations were made. To Leno, Carson was not so much an

idol as the foreman of the most important plant in the business.[1]

To achieve what you want for yourself from your job or career, you may have to work on your career goals as if they were a car! After all, your career is a vehicle that can help take you to your goals, isn't it?

The "Good Employee" Syndrome

If you're like most people, you work for somebody else, which means you are likely to frame your own view and expectations about work around somebody else's expectations of you on the job. You may not even be in touch with what it is you really want out of your professional life because you've always been at the beck and call of somebody else.

I've often encountered this in people who have spent long careers in large corporate bureaucracies. And sometimes in people who are very much oriented to serving the needs of others, like people in nonprofit organizations.

A woman I'll call "Judy" is a highly successful meeting planner for a major trade organization in Alexandria, Virginia. By her own admission, she is a workaholic, often coming in on weekends to complete conference arrangements, handle correspondence, and even do her own secretary's work! "I know I put more into this job than I really should, and I'm not going anywhere in the organization as the result of my efforts," she says. "Part of my problem is that I take too much ownership for what I do, and I know this is hurting my career. Still, it's difficult for me not to give my all to my employer."

Judy has often thought about changing jobs. She's frequently fantasized, for example, about getting into the business of marketing big-name speakers to professional conferences—an activity she has a lot of knowledge of as the result of nearly fifteen years' experience in her field.

Judy keeps in touch with an informal cadre of other meeting planners around town. But she has not yet committed herself emotionally and psychologically to turning her desires into goals. She's still putting the needs of her employer ahead of her own.

What should Judy do? First, she needs to focus on what she wants to do next with her career by outlining some short-, medium-, and long-term goals. Second, she needs to eliminate excuses for not moving forward toward those goals. The best way to do that is to put together a

---

1. Bill Carter, *The Late Shift: Letterman, Leno, and the Network Battle for the Night* (New York: Hyperion, 1994).

career action plan that maps out specific moves she can make toward her goals on a daily basis.

Before you sit down and establish some career goals for yourself, you may need to take the time to develop awareness of what you want to do next. Forget about what your employer might have to say about it! If you tend to get caught up a lot in the "good employee" syndrome, take a day off from work, go walk in the woods, or have an extra-long lunch with a friend. Then grab a scratchpad and ask yourself these questions.

Defining Your Job and Career Goals

1. *Where* do I want to be two, three, five, and ten years from now? Be specific about these short-, medium-, and long-term goals.

    - Two years from now I want. . . .

    - Five years from now I want. . . .

    - Ten years from now I want. . . .

2. *What* do I want to be doing in another job/career? Write a brief description of the ideal job for you.

    My ideal job would enable me to. . . .

3. What skills would it require of me?

4. What do I need to do to position myself for the kind of job/career I really want? Do I need:

    _____ More formal education?
    _____ Specific on-the-job training?
    _____ Additional work experience?
    _____ Formal credentialing of some kind?
    _____ A network of appropriate professional contacts?
    _____ Specific skills I can acquire through self-initiated training or educational efforts?

5. What is it about my background and experience to date that equips me, in some way, for the kind of job or career I want?

6. What in my background/experience not only qualifies me for this kind of job/career, but makes me truly a unique candidate for it?

You'll notice, as you do this exercise, that again you're using the "Going Through Focus" Technique. The power of good questions helps you probe for important answers within yourself, answers that will help you clarify and begin moving toward the goals you want to achieve.

Why is it so important to put your goals down on paper? First, knowing what you want (and what you bring to the table that can help you achieve it) is in many cases half the battle. Indeed, establishing clear and specific goals with specific time frames helps to anchor your career-planning or job exploration efforts.

Second, when you start talking with people about your professional interests, it'll be important to have done some intellectual "spadework"—to have brainstormed about what you want and to have put some preliminary goals in place for discussion with other people.

Finally, committing your goals to paper makes them real and concrete. On this point, I turned from cynic to believer. I used to think that writing down my job/career goals was such a "no-brainer" that I scoffed at its psychological significance for a long time. Then, one time, just for laughs, I committed myself on paper to a series of business and professional goals at the start of the year. And you know what? That year I nearly doubled my income, bought a new home, and accomplished several other things I wanted to do, including paying off all my credit-card debt!

As you begin to develop specific job and career goals, you'll find that the process will fire up your imagination and help get you in gear for the job search or career exploration process. You'll find yourself getting excited about the future because you're doing some highly focused and practical work intended to help you move forward in a proactive way.

You need to know how to remain charged up about going after what you want. The way to do that is to visualize vividly the goals you are striving to reach.

Think about the end result of the goals you are committing yourself to accomplish. What will you gain?

- Increased career satisfaction?
- More money?
- Increased job security?
- A higher professional profile?
- The opportunity to grow and learn professionally?
- The chance to work in a new field or with new and exciting people?

Take a moment now to list all the things that you will gain by committing to and sticking with the career goals you've written down earlier in this chapter.

How do you feel? Don't you feel a sense of warmth inside you? A sense of the possible being attainable?

Now, I want you to imagine what it will be like ten years from now if you don't follow through on your job and career goals. Think how unpleasant and unrewarding your situation will be. Now list these unpleasant consequences.

Sounds like prison, doesn't it? Or like Sartre's famous existential play *No Exit?*

Too many people lock themselves away in jobs that are unsatisfying simply because they never follow through on their dreams and goals; either they don't work up a sufficient head of steam or they conclude that to do so is more effort than they want to expend.

I don't want you to be one of those people!

Believing in the Goodness and Attainability of Your Goals

The second thing that's important in establishing and sticking to goals is believing in the goodness, appropriateness, and attainability of those goals.

Surprisingly, many people don't follow through on goals because they don't feel entitled to anything better for themselves. Sometimes this stems from the person's family experience; perhaps he was not affirmed in going after what he wanted, or perhaps he received "mixed" messages about success and achievement. In chemically dependent households, for example, children often receive conflicting messages about their own self-worth.

In other cases, individuals don't follow through on goals simply because they fear success. The so-called "fear of success" syndrome has been written about a great deal in recent years. It is just as rampant as the fear of failure, but more subtle in nature.

"Georgia" is a single woman in her mid-thirties who is highly computer-literate. She is also very technically oriented. She's built a successful market research career for herself around her use of a computer at work. Although she's very pleasant, Georgia prefers working with her computer over working with other people. This fact makes her a bit uncomfortable at times. "You hear so much about the importance of people being able to work in teams in the workplace today," she told me. "Where does that leave me? Does that make me strange or lacking in social and interpersonal skills?"

Develop a Vision of the Future and an Action Plan to Get You There 53

"Not at all," I told her. "You've been able to function well in teams when that's required of you. You're certainly able to be a team player. It's just that you prefer to work on your own most of the time, to be an individual contributor."

I told Georgia that many people work as individual contributors throughout their careers. "Composers don't write symphonies by committee. Writers don't create story lines for their novels by assembling people in a conference room, and reporters typically don't share their sources with other people at a newspaper or TV station," I pointed out. "So why do you feel you have to always interact with other people in order to be contributing something of worth at work?"

Georgia is a textbook example of somebody who finds it difficult to believe in the appropriateness and the attainability of her own career goals. She's not sure she's entitled to what she wants.

To be successful professionally, you must believe that:

- You are entitled to success.
- Success can be defined in any terms you want.
- Your goals are manifestations of inner yearnings and longings to be more than you are right now.

You must also:

- Be accountable to yourself.
- Eliminate negative or restrictive thinking that stands in the way of taking action.
- Be able to energize yourself to go after what you want.

My friend Rick Dillon is one of the most success-oriented and goal-focused people I know. A square-jawed, salt-of-the-earth kind of guy who happens to work for the federal government, Rick is one of those people who has a perennially optimistic outlook on life. In fact, his optimism is infectious. When you're in the same room with Rick you can't help but think that life is ripe with all kinds of opportunities. One of the things that makes Rick so successful as a human being and that serves as the wellspring of his passion, energy, and interest in other people is that he lives his life close to his heart. In other words, he goes where his energy is. And he goes after what he wants:

> I am a highly energetic, highly motivated person. I do an enormous amount of reading, writing, and networking, which I think is very important in my career. One of the

things I've learned in this proactive life of mine is that you can create opportunities for yourself. Some people, I think, try to tiptoe through life to make it safely to death. But I want to live my life to its fullest. I don't want to die wondering if there were other things I should have done that I didn't attempt.

Rick has learned how to stay fired up about his life and how to keep himself energized in his work on a daily basis. One way he does this is to make himself available to other people who utilize his considerable abilities as a public speaker.

Rick is a consummate public speaker and trainer. He literally sparkles in front of an audience, be it as the emcee of a large group event (he's done a lot of these for the federal government) or as a teacher or trainer in the classroom:

Many of my friends get a rush when they sink a really good putt or hit a golf ball two hundred yards. I get a rush when I am introduced to give a speech or when I walk out in front of an audience. I feel so energized! I've been told that my strength is my ability to communicate. I've been told that by superiors, colleagues, and students.

Rick's ability to energize himself is an important component of career success. He uses the energy and the confidence he derives from public speaking opportunities to fuel longer-term job and career interests. Rick is going to achieve his next career goal—to teach full-time—because he is planning, preparing, and positioning himself for success. He's also going to get there because he *knows what he wants and feels entitled to it!*

If you suffer from a low energy level and lack the energy, drive, or motivation to take more active control of your career, keep the example of Rick Dillon in mind. Also, do this exercise.

Make a list of the kinds of things you enjoy doing. Think about the things you do at work or in your leisure time that really excite and energize you. Are these activities the kinds of things you might be able to incorporate into a job or career? For instance, if you really enjoy writing, perhaps you could do more writing at work. Or perhaps you could create a new job description for yourself, in collaboration with your boss, that utilizes this talent.

Maybe you enjoy being involved in committee activities. If so, perhaps you'd enjoy volunteering to be on a company task force or in a working group. Maybe you want to work in the nonprofit world, where group decision making and consensus building are a large part of getting work done, more so than in private industry.

Maybe there is no readily apparent application in your current job for what you really enjoy doing. Don't fret! This exercise is still important. You need to know the kinds of activities and tasks you enjoy doing, because the things that energize you and give you a sense of identity and purpose also give you self-confidence.

Pursuing Your Career Goals and Dreams One Day at a Time

The third thing that's critical in helping you achieve your goals is striving to reach your goals—one day at a time.

I am a firm believer in the idea that whatever you want professionally you can have—*if* you're willing to pay the price, in terms of planning, preparation, and persistence, to achieve it.

In this regard, being persistent is probably the single most important trait you can cultivate to ensure success.

Though he is often remembered as "Silent Cal," President Calvin Coolidge uttered one of the most memorable statements about the importance of this quality:

> Nothing in the world can take the place of persistence. Talent will not; nothing is more common than unsuccessful men with talent. Genius will not; unrewarded genius is almost a proverb. Education will not; the world is full of educated derelicts. Persistence and determination alone are omnipotent.

One way to be persistent is to pursue your goals one day at a time. Don't think of your job hunt or career transition as a huge long-term project that's impossible to get your hands around. Instead, tackle the tasks at hand by "chunking things down." This will make the challenge seem much more manageable. While it may be tough to envision six months or a year of work in pursuit of your job and career goals, almost anybody can think of following through for just one day (or one week) on pieces of a goal.

Having spent considerable time in twelve-step programs over the years, I can personally attest to the sense of power and control enjoyed by those who have learned to take life one day at a time.

If you think your life is unmanageable at the moment, if you think your career is careening out of control and you are going nowhere fast, think about things you can do—starting now—that will help you lay the foundation for longer-term job and career success.

Developing a Career Action Plan

To get started, put together a career action plan that focuses first on short-term goals and then uses the attainment of these goals as the foundation for medium- and long-term goals.

For example, if you're thinking about changing careers, short-term goals might include:

- Talking with friends, business acquaintances, and others who have made successful job and career transitions
- Researching the field(s) or profession(s) you are interested in
- Doing a personal skills and experience inventory to see how you might leverage your professional background into another field or job
- Taking time out to explore or pursue additional training that will prepare you for a new career down the line, such as getting a professional credential; completing a real-estate or insurance course; taking continuing education courses at a local community college or through a professional organization

If you're interested in staying in the same line of work but think it's time to find another employer, your short-term goals might include:

- Researching specific companies or organizations you might want to work for
- Updating your résumé, fortifying it with concrete and tangible examples of recent professional accomplishments you've had on the job
- Networking actively through friends, colleagues, and professional groups to unearth job leads and learn who in your city or community is hiring and whom you might position yourself with for informational interviews
- Assessing whether there are other professional opportunities with your employer that are worth exploring

Your career action plan will be the roadmap by which you move forward. It's designed to give you a framework for preparing for a job or career transition by helping you focus on your goals, build momentum for achieving what you want, and moving from "notion to motion" with your career plans.

From Notion to Motion: Moving From Goals to Action

Look at the diagram in Figure 4-1. At the bottom of the pyramid (Level One) are your personal desires and dreams that relate to your career. Perhaps this is where you were when you picked up this book. You had some hopes and dreams about doing something more satisfying with your career, but you hadn't really begun to focus yet on what those ideas were. They were vague and abstract. Moreover, there was no energy or focus behind attaining these things for yourself.

Or perhaps you were at Level Two. You had some specific ideas about what you wanted to do (perhaps the basic concept for a business of your own), but you didn't really know how to translate those ideas into actions that would result in success.

This exercise will help you harness the self-awareness, self-confidence, and sense of purpose you need to move toward the achievement of your career goals and dreams. In essence, you're going to begin building up the head of steam necessary to proceed from Level Three (Goals, Objectives, Plans) to the highest levels of this pyramid—to your

Figure 4-1. The career planning pyramid.

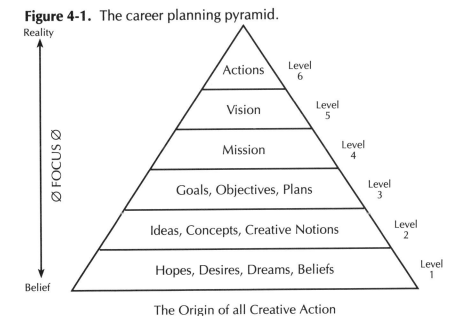

The Origin of all Creative Action

career mission and vision and to the actions that will help you turn these things into reality.

After you outline your short-, medium-, and long-term goals, you're going to develop personal career mission and vision statements that will represent the encapsulation of those personal goals.

Your Career Mission and Vision

What is a career mission and vision, anyway?

Webster's Dictionary defines *mission* as "that which one is destined or fitted to do; a calling." What do you desire or feel called to do with your job and career? For many people, developing a career mission statement entails finding a way to be of service to others.

The *Oxford American Dictionary* defines *vision* as "something seen in the imagination or in a dream." Typically, there is a quality of the ideal about a vision. Think, then, of your career vision as your dream job toward which you are going to aim all of your personal and creative action, passion, and energy in the days, weeks, and months ahead.

As you complete this exercise, you may want to consult the list of sample goals included in this chapter. Take care in answering the following questions. The more complete you can be, the more focused and energized you will be as you work through subsequent chapters. Where appropriate, integrate answers from the exercises in Chapters 1, 2, and 3.

Creating Your Career Action Plan

1. Develop a list of short-term job and career goals for yourself (time frame for completion: one to six months).
2. Which of these goals can you move forward to accomplish immediately?
3. Prioritize your short-term goals.
4. Develop a list of your medium-term goals (time frame for completion: six months to one year).
5. Which of these goals can you begin working on immediately?
6. Prioritize your medium-term goals.
7. Develop a list of your long-term goals (time frame for completion: more than one year).
8. Which of these goals can you begin work on immediately?
9. Prioritize your long-term goals.
10. On the basis of your answers to questions 1–9, develop a job and career vision statement.

Develop a Vision of the Future and an Action Plan to Get You There   59

11. On the basis of those same answers, develop a career mission statement.

Examples of Job and Career Goals

Short-Term Goals

- Research the job market in areas of interest to you. Municipal and college libraries are good places to start.
- Research educational requirements, formal credentials, and certification that may be necessary to enter the field. Contact professional societies and associations that represent the professions or industries you are interested in for information.
- Arrange to meet with people who are further along in your profession or who have made successful transitions into other fields.
- Begin thinking about how your skills and professional background might provide you with pivot points for moving into another job or career. Make a list of these potential pivot points.
- Dust off and update your résumé to include some accomplishments and functional strengths you've used in the recent past. Keep in mind that for purposes of planning a move ahead in your current field, you'll most likely use a chronological résumé format. For purposes of moving into other fields, you'll want to use a functional résumé format (more about résumés in Chapter 6).
- Take time to catalogue and become conversant with your skills, talents, experience, and accomplishments. Build on exercises you did in Chapter 3.
- If interested, seek some career or vocational testing. Local colleges and universities are a good source of information and services. Testing is probably appropriate if you are uncertain of what you want or if finding good job "fit" has historically been difficult for you. In addition, organizations such as the Capability Corporation, based in Spokane, Washington, will, on a dial-up basis, provide you with analyses of how you can transfer your skills to other industries.
- Read at least one book a month that relates to jobs, careers, and the changing American workplace. Go to the self-help/business section of your local bookstore for a collection of up-to-date titles.
- Keep an eye out for magazines that contain good articles on planning and managing your career. Examples include: *Working*

Woman, New Woman, Men's Health, Men's Fitness, Harvard Business Review, BusinessWeek and *Forbes*.
- Consider seeking counseling from a certified therapist, social worker, or psychologist/psychiatrist if you think there are issues you need to address in the areas of success, goal setting, personal entitlement, or self-esteem.

Medium-Term Goals

- Compile a list of people who can be of help to you in your job-hunting or career-exploration process. Individuals can include: friends, relatives, neighbors, business associates, your lawyer, doctor, or accountant, coworkers, former bosses, other people you know who have changed jobs/careers, people you know through church or synagogue, alumni and alumna groups, and professional organizations.
- Make a commitment to meet with the people on this list within a specific period of time to help you gain clarity about your job and career objectives.
- Develop a list of target companies and organizations that may be of interest for you to explore.
- Do some in-depth research on prospective companies and organizations using the library and various online computer database services now available. Numerous database research services are available today. Career Search contains information on more than 200,000 public and private companies. The High Technology Marketplace Database and Fax-on-Demand, a service that will fax you information on prospective employers within half an hour, are other good sources of employer profile information.
- Make plans to complete a partially finished undergraduate or graduate degree.

Long-Term Goals

- Find a job in a new company, organization, industry, or field.
- Complete an undergraduate or graduate-level degree program that will foster your long-term job and career objectives.
- Consider relocation to another geographical area if it will position you for job opportunities in a new and emerging field or industry.
- Develop additional subject matter expertise in your current field or in another area of interest.

HABIT #5

Learn to Work "Smart" Where You Are Right Now

> This time, like all times, is a very good one, if we but know what to do with it.
>
> —Ralph Waldo Emerson

A lot of us were raised with naïve and pristine notions about the way things are supposed to work at work. The Puritan work ethic, for example, suggests that doing a good job is its own reward, and a lot of people still subscribe to the idea that if you simply concentrate on doing your job, other people will recognize, reward, and acknowledge you for your efforts.

Unfortunately, thinking this way nowadays can do you a disservice rather than help you look after your professional interests.

Today, knowing how to blow your own horn and how to position yourself effectively within an organization are critical to your career success. If carefully cultivated, these skills can help rocket your career into high orbit and set you apart from the vast mass of other jobholders out there.

Positioning Yourself for Success

I hope by this time it's clear that to be a successful professional in today's business environment, you need more than skills and talent. You also need well-honed political and interpersonal skills, a good sense of timing, an intuitive sense of how to work with people, and an ability to read the organizational entrails where you work.

You don't have to be a cold-blooded sociopath, a ruthless turf builder, or a backstabbing gossipmonger to get ahead in today's workplace. But you do need to know how to demonstrate your professional value to your boss or organization. Moreover, you need to be shrewd, deliberate, and purposeful in planning and managing professional moves up the ladder or through the organizational maze.

How do you become your own press agent, advocate, lobbyist, and publicist within an organization without being viewed as simply a self-serving opportunist? Start by becoming smart about the place where you work.

Rule #1: Become "Maze-Bright" About the Place Where You Work

Often we believe that once we are inside an organization, someone (a boss or mentor perhaps) will be there to help us climb the professional ladder. Indeed, we assume that if we do a good job, we will be promoted and pushed upward and onward through an organization. Yet today there's a good chance your own boss is too preoccupied with his own job security and the shifting organizational sands beneath his feet to think much about helping you chart and navigate the channels leading to advancement in your organization.

As for mentors, they are wonderful when you can find them. But the rapid pace of change in many businesses today can cause the "org" charts to be rewritten overnight, sweeping away organizational proximity or chains of command that made mentor-protégé relationships possible in the first place. I know because it once happened to me. I had a very supportive and mentoring boss who was replaced by somebody else who told me the company had no time to mentor its employees!

For these reasons, it's critical that you become "maze-bright" about your organization. Don't hide behind your desk. Instead, make it a point to develop a sense of where the organization is going. Is it developing a new "mission and vision" for the future, for instance? Understand and "manage" your boss effectively, and identify key players who will have roles to play in your organization's future.

Rule #2: Become an Industry Watcher and Trend Tracker

Keep track of trends in the business marketplace, in the economy, or in the international arena that might impact your job, your organization, or your industry. Developing a global perspective on the work your organization does is critically important if you want to be savvy about the future of your organization or industry.

As part of this process, ask yourself questions like these:

- What's the future of my industry? Is it growing, shrinking, dying?
- Is the industry evolving into something else? Something exciting? Something I'd like to be part of? Or not?
- What's the future of the job I am doing right now? Given developments in technology, the growing global economy, and this organization, is my job function likely to be critical to this organization in the years ahead?
- Have I been rewarded and recognized for making a critical contribution to the organization's success, or do I mostly get paternalistic pats on the back?
- Is the skill-set required to do this job changing? Is this a skill-set I'm interested in using and upgrading over time?

Rule #3: Assess the Realistic Prospects for Promotion and Advancement Where You Are Right Now

Think realistically about what you believe your long-term prospects for advancement and further professional development to be within your organization—even in other job functions.

Unfortunately, the glass (and concrete) ceilings are still alive and functioning in much of the American workplace. A 1991 study conducted by the U.S. Department of Labor concluded that:

> If there is not, in fact, a glass ceiling [in corporate America] there certainly is a point beyond which minorities and women have not advanced in many companies. Secondly, minorities have plateaued at lower levels of the workforce than women. [And] monitoring for equal access and opportunity, especially as managers move up the corporate ladder to senior management levels where important decisions are made, is almost never considered a corporate responsibility or part of the planning for developmental programs and policies.[1]

For these reasons, check out your organization's commitment to diversity. If you're an African-American woman, find out your organization's track record on promoting women and minorities. Is there a strong commitment to the advancement of women in the workplace, or does your employer make only a token effort to promote women and

---

1. "A Report on the Glass Ceiling Initiative," U.S. Department of Labor, 1991, p. 4.

minorities? If you're interested in reading more about career issues for African-American women, pick up a copy of *Work Sister Work: Why Black Women Can't Get Ahead and What They Can Do About It* by Leslie and Cydney Shields. Also, check out the Catalyst organization in New York.

If you're gay or lesbian and are concerned about how disclosure of information about your sexuality to your employer would likely impact your career prospects in your organization, check out your company's equal employment opportunity protection statement to see if sexual orientation is covered. Many gays and lesbians feel that, with the exception of a few record companies and hair salons, most employers are still living in the late Middle Ages when it comes to issues of sexual orientation. But you'll be interested to know that an increasing number of organizations—Lotus, Levi Strauss, AT&T, MCI, Fannie Mae, and Apple Computer, among others—have made efforts to be more inclusive and protective of gay and lesbian employees, and others are slowly following suit. Apple and Fannie Mae are two companies that provide spousal benefits to same-sex couples.

Trust your gut on the issue of disclosing your sexuality in the workplace. It may matter a great deal to you that others in your workplace know about your private life; on the other hand, you may feel it is nobody's business but your own. The only definitive thing I have to say about this is that the decision is a uniquely personal one. An article in the *Harvard Business Review* entitled "Is This the Right Time to Come Out At Work" (July–August 1993) suggests that the time may be coming when it will be easier to be "out" at work than it is today. For more information on this topic, you may also want to read Brian McNaught's book, *Gay Issues in the Workplace*.

Rule #4: Determine if Your Work Style and Work Values Match Those of Your Employer

Are your personal and your work styles in sync with those of your organization? While some degree of conformity is part of working in any organization, take stock of whether your job requires you to check your identity at the door. Human beings are called upon to be adaptable at work, but you shouldn't have to struggle. If you're a working mother, for example, and your company isn't very "family-friendly"—doesn't provide day care services or make it easy for you to balance job and family demands—I'd think about working someplace else. If you're an African-American man who's tried unsuccessfully to break into the senior sales management ranks of your company, maybe it's time to look for an organization that's going to value you for the diversity you bring to the organization.

Some organizations make a very active attempt to recruit a wide variety of workers and fly the diversity "banner" proudly. Prospect Associates, a health sciences research and communications firm based in Rockville, Maryland, includes employee profile information in its marketing brochure:

> Prospect actively seeks diversity in our workplace and staff capabilities. The versatility and diversity of our staff are reflected in the demographic makeup, breadth of academic disciplines, and variety of work experience among our employees. Prospect has employment opportunities for those newly entering their profession as well as those who have established reputations in their respective fields.

Rule #5: Determine if Your Employer Is Committed to Developing You

Increasingly, it's being recognized that investing in people is a sound way for a company to build a competitive business posture in the marketplace. Unfortunately, many organizations and bosses have not yet awakened to this fact. Check out your organization's commitment to employee development and training. Ask yourself:

- What kinds of training and development programs does this organization offer?
- Am I encouraged to take advantage of these programs, or is it difficult for me to get time off to attend them?
- How interested is my boss in helping me grow and develop my skills?
- Does my employer offer tuition reimbursement for courses taken and requirements fulfilled toward an M.B.A. or other business graduate programs?
- Are there opportunities for me to develop on the job through job rotation, task force assignments, special projects, and lateral transfers? Or am I effectively trapped in a box?

Rule #6: Assess Your Relationship With Your Current Boss

As a matter of courtesy, ethics, professionalism, and practicality, you need to assess the environment where you work by looking at the relationship you have with your boss. Is he/she:

- A professional colleague for whom you feel great respect and with whom you feel a strong professional chemistry?
- A savvy political operator within the organization with whom you feel you can effectively work, even though your styles and areas of expertise may be quite different?
- A power tripper or control freak who's more interested in being your gatekeeper and supervisor than in co-creating a professional relationship and recognizing your competence and expertise?
- A well-meaning but organizationally ineffective manager who lacks the respect of his/her peers and supervisors?
- An inept or incompetent individual who knows nothing about what you do and isn't interested in learning and who appears to be a lousy organizational political player as well?

Once you've determined the kind of boss you have, you can put together a game plan for dealing effectively with this person. (See Exhibit 5-1.)

Professional Colleague?

If your boss is for all intents and purposes your professional equal, you may be able to discuss quite openly and candidly what your career goals and objectives are. Because this person may also be a friend, the opportunity may exist for the two of you to explore ways you can continue working together in the future or how you might be able to expand or enrich your current job responsibilities to include more challenging assignments and projects.

Your boss may be able to suggest ways you could get cross-functional or cross-department experience in your organization, perhaps by working for her professional peer or through informal networking.

The best boss I ever had was a woman who supervised me when I was with AT&T. We weren't even located in the same city, yet we worked well together, discussing business several times a week during conference calls. There was an implicit trust and respect between us that resulted from more than chemistry. I worked long hours on many occasions for Judith (she was the kind of boss I would have crossed rivers for) and felt good about it. The reason? I knew she respected me as a professional. She also was willing to go to the mat for me and demonstrated an interest and concern for my own career growth and satisfaction.

Exhibit 5-1. Your boss and his or her role in your career.

Your boss. He may be the joy of your life or the bane of your existence—or perhaps both. We all have bosses to contend with, and they can have a definite impact, for better or worse, on our careers.

So how do you involve your boss in your career plans?

First, you have to determine what kind of boss you have. Is she supportive of you and your aspirations, or is she more interested in keeping you chained to your desk, doing her work? The following exercise will help you determine the kind of boss you work for.

Workplace Reality Check

Use the following questions to identify the "descriptors" that best apply to your boss.

Is your boss:

- A motivator who empowers you on the job?
- A team player who considers herself a member of the team and who makes a deliberate effort to create a close and cohesive team structure in the workplace?
- A self-appointed babysitter who feels his most important role is to supervise you?
- A micromanager who's always in your hair and who constantly questions your judgment about things?
- A gatekeeper/idea spoiler who nay-says most of your suggestions and initiatives or ignores them altogether?
- An information hoarder who keeps you in the dark about business decisions and what he is thinking?
- An in-house politician whose only vision seems to be to look upward in the organization and who never seems to see, much less acknowledge, her employees?
- A dictator who wants you to always remember that you work for her?
- A control freak who can't delegate, doesn't trust, and questions everything you and your coworkers advocate, recommend, or lobby for?
- A martyr who's always playing for sympathy and who's able to manipulate you as a result?
- Other (specify)

(continues)

Exhibit 5-1. (continued)

The kind of boss you work for dictates how open and straightforward you are about discussing your career goals. With a good boss, you can share a lot about your goals and dreams. He, in fact, can be a partner in the career planning process. Unfortunately, there are a lot of poor bosses out there who are antediluvian in their management thinking, who, out of ignorance, lack of interest, or shortsightedness, can have a negative impact on your career unless you recognize them for what they are and plan accordingly—by seizing the day and becoming your own career coach!

Tom Morris, president of Morris Associates, a career counseling firm, says that dealing with the "B factor," as he calls it, is critical if you want to become more empowered in managing your career. He says that your boss may not actively help you develop professionally because she:

- May not be comfortable interacting with you on a roughly equal (e.g., one adult to another) or collegial basis.
- May not, by nature, be a good trainer, listener, communicator, or coach.
- May have only a narrow field of professional experience; in fact, her professional perspective and outlook may not be as broad or sophisticated as your own.
- May have a rigid and hidebound outlook on subordinates (they're to be supervised) and on work.
- May tend to follow the dictates of company policy to the letter and have little interest in or imagination regarding ways to be a more effective boss.
- May not want to change.
- May not want you to change.
- May not see the bottom-line benefit of helping you develop in your career (a.k.a. "What's in it for me?").
- May not have thought about helping you.

You don't want someone else's lack of vision, interest, or imagination keeping you from doing what you want and moving forward, do you? Don't defer career plans or goals to a boss. Work with him if possible, but don't let him be a roadblock in your professional life.

Savvy Political Operator?

If your boss tends to be a savvy political operator within the organization, you may still be able to talk quite openly together about your professional goals and receive support from him. Unlike the first type of boss, however, a political operator usually offers less of a personal connection. He will probably suggest other people in the organization with whom you might be able to forge strong professional connections and will see this kind of "referral to other sources" as a part of his responsibility to you. This kind of boss has his own personal agenda, which may or may not include you. Trust your instincts in terms of how much you share and what you rely on this person for. I suggest you approach career discussions with this kind of boss in a straightforward, professional way. Solicit ideas, support, and guidance about how you can effectively position yourself for future career success within the organization. This will most likely strike a hot button with this boss, who prides himself on his organizational and political savvy.

Power Tripper, Gatekeeper, Control Freak?

If you work for somebody like this, be very cautious about sharing your personal career plans and goals with her. This kind of person is often insecure, tends to be intrusive, presumptuous, and "parental" in her treatment of employees, and tries to establish a "parent-child" relationship with you, in many cases through manipulation. Social worker Kathy Hower has observed that bosses like this are often paranoid and have high control needs, which makes working for them a constant minefield:

> Even if you do an outstanding job for a boss like this, you're likely to be 'punished' for it in some way. Bosses like this are fearful of too much competence in their employees. Thus, they will undermine you, question every decision you make, and never afford you much professional purview or respect in the workplace.

The Boss From Hell?

The worst boss I ever had was a fellow like this. He micromanaged his employees. He was a little Caesar who did not command respect so much as demand attention. Moreover, his need for control was so great that he used to stipulate how far employees' desks could be from the wall. And while he gave lip service to collegiality and consensus building, he was a "top-down" manager if ever I saw one. Today, in retrospect, I realize that in this guy's mind, my "calves were too fat." In other words, I couldn't click my boots together as quickly as he might have wished. Ultimately, being competent mattered less to this guy than realizing that you were his subordinate.

If you work for a control freak, assess your own career interests, then cultivate a professional network of contacts that does not include your supervisor. You might, for instance, build relationships with peers, coworkers, and colleagues in other parts of your office or organization who can be affirming of you and who can provide you with a reality check on what may be happening to you in your office.

Be cautious, however, about sharing too much with in-house contacts, acquaintances, and associates, particularly if you work for a small organization or in one where the grapevine flourishes.

Develop your deepest professional friendships outside your organization. These contacts can provide you with important feedback about yourself independent of the place where you're working. That's extremely important information and perspective to acquire, especially if you work in a dysfunctional organization or in one where the communication is very poor.

Is there any way to thrive while working for a boss who is a control freak? Even though you may be working in an unpleasant and even toxic work environment, try to complete tasks and projects that are important to you, and look for ways to leverage these things to your advantage, perhaps as new bullet items on your résumé.

At the same time, try to detach yourself emotionally from the chaos around you. My good friend and professional colleague Matt Whalen suggests that one way to find serenity or at least to detach from workplace confusion and tension is to picture yourself at the center of a hurricane lamp, safely shielded from the howling gales around you:

> At the office picture yourself as a flame, surrounded by a transparent barrier of protection that keeps the wind and the toxic elements of your work environment away from you. Within the center, the area of protection, you can then function and retain a consistency of performance, even though the winds of organizational chaos and dysfunction may be swirling all around you.

Organizationally Ineffective?

One of the nicest bosses I ever had was also one who was probably the least effective organizationally. He was not well respected by his colleagues. This had less to do, I think, with his competence than with the culture of the organization in which we were working.

Eventually, Phil got canned from his job. I liked Phil a great deal. One of his finest qualities was that he was very democratic in his dealings with subordinates, perhaps too much so from the point of view of his peers in the organization.

If you work for a boss like this, you need to build political links with others in the organization and maintain loyalty to your boss at the same time. He may be of benefit to you, even if he is not ultimately effective on his own behalf. The fact is, Phil helped me advance in my career.

If your boss is like Phil, be a class act. Don't talk about him behind his back. If, in building alliances or relationships with others in your organization, you find that others bash or criticize your boss, weigh what is being said in the context of the moment. Is it a throwaway comment, or does it appear to be part of a character assassination campaign?

An Incompetent Boob Without Knowing It?

As somebody who's worked for at least two incompetent bosses in his career, I suggest you do what's expected of you but no more. She lacks the vision to use you or help you develop to your fullest, but she is probably arrogant and insecure enough to make your life a living hell if you're not careful. Therefore, you have to become (and remain) self-energized in order to pursue your goals. Expect no help from an incompetent boss. Indeed, she may feel a vested interest in keeping you corralled in a job in her own work group, if for no other reason than that counting you as part of her office headcount helps legitimate her own job to upper management.

Like control freaks, incompetent bosses tend to micromanage their employees. If this occurs, resist the temptation (tough if you take pride and ownership in the work you do) to let your self-esteem be battered and bruised by a boss who harangues you and is all over you and your work.

Keep your spirits up, network elsewhere within the organization, and actively seek out other potential bosses. You must do this discreetly, but you may find entrée to prospective bosses through mentors or co-workers.

Rule #7: Look for Ways to Enhance Your Job Security in Today's Organizational Environment

You may be happily employed with your company and feel secure. You may even worship the ground your boss walks on. It does happen. But don't get too comfortable or complacent—you could be blindsided someday.

If, for instance, you never develop any contacts outside your immediate department, what would you do if your boss announced that he was taking early retirement? If you had no other ties to similar levels of management in your organization, you could be at the mercy of your boss's replacement.

I suggest, therefore, that you take the following preemptive steps to enhance your chances of staying with your company even if layoffs and departmental downsizing occur down the road.

- *Think of yourself as being in business for yourself.* In Chapter 1, I mentioned the importance of doing this as a means of taking greater responsibility for managing your career, because it puts the onus on you to perform in your present job while forcing you to keep abreast of developments in your organization that could impact you. It also conditions you to see yourself as a professional in your field, rather than as simply an employee. This helps build a layer of protection around your sense of professional identity, which can be a plus in times of stress and organizational change. Tom Peters calls this developing a "consultant's mind-set" about your work. In today's volatile organizational environments, it's critical for professionals to do—because bosses will come and go.

- *Know what you have contributed to your organization.* Keep a running list of your professional accomplishments throughout the year. Set up a file in your PC to keep track of projects you've been involved in or other things that demonstrate your contributions. Doing this on a regular basis makes you aware of your value to your company. At the end of the year, incorporate these things into an updated internal company résumé. Also, work them up in an appropriate format for use in an external résumé. You never know when you might want to send your internal résumé to somebody in another part of the company or float your external résumé in the open job market.

- *Don't cocoon yourself in your office.* A lot of people tend to cocoon themselves at work, limiting their contacts in the organization to a small clutch or coffee klatch of coworkers. This is particularly the case in large bureaucracies, such as federal or state government agencies and departments.

But nowadays this isn't smart to do. Instead, make yourself known to other people in the organization. If you work in accounting, operations, or other internally oriented departments or functional areas, for example, make a particular effort to get to know people in other departments.

This is critically important, because people who work in internal staff jobs in organizations frequently have smaller and less diverse professional contact networks than do other professionals—people in sales, marketing, public relations, external affairs, and so forth.

Also, if your company has branches in different cities and states, try to position yourself to visit other locations from time to time, and get to know the people in these areas. As a colleague of mine who works for the federal government says:

> In big bureaucracies it's really easy to become invisible and to feel like you are not making a difference.
>
> I think people choose to become invisible and therefore don't make a difference. You can either melt into the woodwork, or you can publicize the issues you care about, the things you know about, make yourself an expert on certain things, and manipulate the bureaucracy in ways to further your visibility.

- *Attach yourself to a rising star.* Pick out some rising stars in your company, people you'd like to emulate or who work in an emerging new area of focus. Don't worry that they're higher up in the organization than you. Maybe you can serve on an interdepartmental committee with them, or kibbitz with them in the company gym. What you want to do is make yourself visible to others so that they'll know who you are should the time come when you need to find a new place in the organization to call home. (*Hint:* Marketing is often hiring, even in the leanest of times.) But be subtle about your activities. Your goal isn't to job-hop right now. Rather, it's to build a professional network of people in the organization who know you and your abilities.

- *Cultivate good relations with support people.* In my experience, one of the most overlooked and undervalued resources in most offices is the support staff that works with executives and managers. If properly cultivated as friends and coworkers, members of your support staff or administrative group can be extremely valuable to you professionally, if for no other reason than that they will generate positive word-of-mouth about you. "Jack," a high-level manager in the federal government, says:

> I think that if you overlook the clerical and administrative people in your organization, you are destined to flop. There are very strong networks of clerical and administrative people

who communicate among themselves, particularly in a large organization. These are people who can sabotage your work as it flows through the organization. In many cases, they are the people who literally carry your work from one level to another. And if they don't like you, if you're rude to or dismissive of them, they will ditch your work, or you will find that somehow it gets 'lost' in somebody's in-box.

Jack fosters a close bond with support people. He helps them move forward with their careers, specifically by helping them complete the complicated S-171 form that is required of all government employees.

"I've worked with at least a dozen people over the years when they've applied for new jobs," he says. "That's never forgotten. People in the bureaucracy at the administrative and clerical level are very good to me because they know I'm looking out for them."

• *Commit yourself to continuous learning and professional development.* One of the best ways to keep yourself attractive to any employer is to keep your skills up to date. If you're a middle manager whose main job has been managing other people, take time to brush up on or revive your hands-on technical skills. If you've never learned to use a computer, learn now. (See Chapter 11.)

Rule #8: Learn to Spot the Warning Signs That Your Job Is in Trouble

There are some loud signals you can pick up on in the office that will indicate whether your job is in jeopardy. Ask yourself these questions:

1. *Has your company been acquired by a corporate raider?* If it has, chances are a big organizational shakeup will soon follow, and a lot of jobs may be axed. Even if you've been doing a great job and your boss loves your work—watch out. There's a good chance your job duplicates what somebody in the takeover company is already doing. And that means that somebody is likely to be shown the door in the near future—probably you; you may be declared "redundant" to the organization.

2. *Is that new boss of yours (the third one you've had in as many months) known as a ruthless budget slasher?* Is she telling everybody at staff meetings that the company can't afford to give employees free coffee anymore? If your new supervisor is carving up your department's budget as if it were a pork roast, eliminating training money or slashing

travel, for example, take note. Chances are that higher-level management is putting the squeeze on her to cut expenses. Staff cuts are probably not far behind.

3. *Did you get a rude awakening at your last performance review?* Did you slip from being "outstanding" in your boss's mind to being somebody who isn't performing up to par or who isn't toeing the line? When companies are on the verge of layoffs, they often do a rating and ranking of employees to determine who stays and who goes. Sometimes where you fall in the scheme of things is based a lot more on politics than on performance. If all of a sudden you begin to get bad reviews for your work—even when your work has always been rated good or better—it may be a signal that layoffs are imminent.

4. *What else is going on around the office that seems to be out of the ordinary?* When companies are about to downsize and lay people off, you can often pick up what I call "organizational body language" that indicates what's in the offing.

Are the top managers out of the office more than usual, sequestered at headquarters for what seems to be an endless series of meetings? They may be doing a head count of who is to be cut. Is the copy machine putting in overtime as it cranks out résumés for all the secretaries in the office and the ones next door? That's a sure sign that something's up. What about staff changes? Do you get an updated organization chart in your in-box just about every week? Finally, have key projects of yours been nixed or put on hold? All these things are indicators that your company is in transition and may be consolidating operations or lines of business.

Don't get paranoid about what's happening in your office, but do be alert to what's occurring around you. Pay attention to the signals you get from upper management, and stay as close to your boss as you can. Pump him for information, and voice your concerns. A good boss will pick up on these things and be as honest and direct with you as possible about what's happening.

Rule #9: Treat Internal Company Interviews Like Any Other Interview—PREPARE FOR THEM

You've seen it coming for a long time. Your company has finally made the decision to downsize and consolidate operations, but you're not worried. You're a shoo-in (you tell yourself) for that job in marketing, operations, or management information systems (MIS).

Or are you?

People who work for large corporations sometimes assume (unfortunately) that if their department downsizes or goes away entirely they'll be able to make a soft landing elsewhere in the organization with just a single phone call. But even the best networking in the world doesn't normally happen this quickly.

If you find yourself called for internal company interviews, don't assume you've got the job ahead of time, just because you know the person doing the interviewing. And even if you're told you've got the job, don't let this disarm you. You never know who might be in line behind you who's got things to offer—and who isn't assuming ahead of time that he or she has the job.

Prepare for an internal company interview just as you would for any other interview. Do some information gathering ahead of time. If the job is in the same location as where you are now, you might hand-deliver the résumé to the person who'll be interviewing you. This will give you a chance to discreetly check out the work area and who else is part of that person's department. Do you know others in the work group? Grab them for lunch in the company cafeteria, have coffee with them in the canteen, or take a walk with them around the company grounds.

Find out as much about the job as you can. Why is it available at this time? Who was in it before? What's your prospective boss like to work for? Find out if there's been a lot of turnover in the position. And find out how other people in the department feel about the person you'd be reporting to. Is she a saint to work for, or more like Saddam Hussein or Leona Helmsley?

Here are other things you need to know. Is the job new or existing? What's the scope of responsibility? Is travel involved? If so, how much? If you move over from another department, will the move be lateral or promotional?

Don't assume that just because it's a higher-level job, you'll be automatically promoted. Your organization may try to stick you with a new job title but keep you at your current salary grade. If it tries this, make a case for the fact that you have a lot to offer and see the new job as a logical progression in your career path.

As for the interview itself, write out questions you have about the position ahead of time, and ask them in the interview. Also, prep yourself to answer questions. Besides talking about your strengths and accomplishments, be ready to talk about how you would handle different situations should they arise on the job.

This point is critical. A lot of interviewers ask questions designed to get at the thinking processes of the people they interview. They'll ask questions such as "Tell me how you would handle things if you were faced with the following situation" or "Talk to me about what you would do if given the choice between A and B."

Anticipate questions like this. They require you to articulate how you would handle yourself on the job, and they're intended to get at not only your underlying thought processes but your philosophy of work. You may not be expecting them when you walk in the door for the interview, but interviewers increasingly use them to get a handle on a person's on-the-job work experience and decision-making style.

Finally, don't be too familiar with the interviewer, even if you already know him or her. That is, don't put your feet on the desk, and don't be too relaxed. And, once the interview is over, do send a thank-you note. Don't send it through the company mail; drop it in a mailbox with a stamp.

Do these things, and you will definitely stand out from other internal job candidates. They can make the difference between getting the job and being the interviewer's second choice.

Positioning Yourself for Success if Your Current Job Goes Away

Up to this point in this chapter, I've talked about all the things you can do to position yourself for success in your current organization and how, in many cases, you can enhance your job security for the long term.

In this era of downsizings and corporate restructurings, however, it's likely that at some point in your career you will face an involuntary separation from your employer. If that happens, what will you feel? Will you be able to deal with the impact of a layoff?

In Chapter 6, I deal with these issues and with how you can effectively package yourself for professional success during an external job hunt or career transition.

HABIT #6

Always Be Prepared for the External Job Market

> The meeting of preparation with opportunity generates the offspring we call luck.
>
> —Anthony Robbins

Losing a job is one of the most stressful things that can happen to anybody. In fact, it's number three on the "stress" list after the death of a loved one and divorce.

But in today's economy, job loss continues to be common. As of this writing, Phillip Morris has just announced plans to lay off fourteen thousand workers, and predictions are that downsizings will continue to be a major news item for the next several years at the very least.

Rule #1: Let Yourself Have Feelings About the Experience

If you find yourself laid off or outpaced, the first thing you need to do is acknowledge your feelings of loss. This is not the time for a stiff upper lip. Your job defines much of your personal identity, especially in this culture, where there is so much emphasis on professionalism and achievement. Consequently, when you lose a job you may experience a roller coaster of feelings—grief, anger, relief, resentment, depression, denial, and eventually acceptance. It's important to acknowledge your feelings and to express them to a spouse, partner, counselor if necessary, and certainly friends. Dealing with feelings—not "stuffing" them—is the way to move on.

Rule #2: Don't Jump at Just Any Job

During this period of time, be careful. Don't act like a jilted lover and simply go out and take another job (any job) on the rebound. You'll probably regret it. For example, don't rush out and in a fit of pique plunk down $20,000 for a franchise—until you've had time to sort through your feelings, determine some goals, and think about the options you really want to explore.

I've known twenty-year veterans of big companies, for instance, who've gone out and negotiated shaky arrangements to join start-up companies without giving themselves adequate time to grieve the loss of their previous employment relationship. They move too fast and without doing adequate research about the nature of work in a start-up company. Believe me, it's a far cry from working for a *Fortune* 500 company.

In other cases, I've seen people embark upon job searches without adequately processing the anger or sense of inadequacy they feel as a result of having been laid off. The consequence is that their anger and insecurity get in the way of their being able to move on to new things and become roadblocks that prospective employers often pick up on in informational or job interviews.

Instead of acting rashly, take time to map out your plans and decide what you want to do next.

Do you want to stay in the same line of work, or is it time to explore opportunities in other industries? Maybe you've been a lawyer for twenty years and want to embark now on that long-delayed (but often dreamed-about) career as a business consultant. Maybe you fantasize about doing something really offbeat, like becoming an organic gardener, editor of an antiques magazine, or one of those disembodied voices that does television voiceovers.

Whatever you decide, do some homework to see if there are job opportunities out there for you, or opportunities that you can reasonably create for yourself.

Rule #3: Become an Information Hound

For starters, get a subscription to *The National Business Employment Weekly*. It's an essential primer on the world of job search and career transition, containing a rich mix of articles on everything from how to interview successfully to how to research job opportunities. NBEW also does an excellent job of projecting where—in terms of both geography and industry—you can find jobs for the future.

Check out business news magazines to keep abreast of trends and developments in the workplace and to keep a pulse on industries that are hot. Magazines such as *Working Woman* and *U.S. News and World*

Report publish annual job and career guides that showcase hot industries and jobs, complete with business and employment forecasts.

Then, of course, there are some marvelous new books that talk about the changing nature of jobs in different professions.

If you're a banker, you may want to pick up a copy of *Career Alternatives for Bankers* by William King, Dean Graber, and Rebecca Newton. Once considered among the most secure and placid of professions, banking has undergone radical transformation in recent years as "megabanks" have gobbled up smaller institutions, forcing the layoff of thousands of people. This book is an excellent resource for anyone who wants to stay in this shrinking field or who is open to exploring options tangential to banking—with banking "outsourcers" and financial services firms, for example.

If you're a young lawyer interested in scoping out the organizational culture of law firms, pick up a copy of *The Insider's Guide to Law Firms, 1993–1994*. Written by law students, it contains a wealth of information on hundreds of law firms in twelve U.S. cities, spelling out things like the starting salaries for associates, the kinds of pro bono work each firm does, and the nature of relationships between associates and partners.

Maybe what really turns you on is the new and emerging field of environmental engineering and waste management. In that case, get a hold of *The New Complete Guide to Environmental Careers*. It contains information on careers in everything from parks and outdoor recreation to air and water quality control, hazardous waste management, land and water conservation, and solid waste management.

Finally, if you get turned on by job research itself, get a copy of *Researching Your Way to a Good Job* by Karmen Crowther. It looks at the exploding number of on-line databases and compact disc programs and services that are available to assist job seekers in doing job-market research and in getting their résumés into the right "electronic" hands.

Rule #4: Package Yourself for Success With Your Résumé

It doesn't matter whether you're a career veteran with twenty years of working experience or a student with a fresh degree; your résumé is the cornerstone of any job-search/career-transition strategy. So take time and pains to prepare it carefully.

Deciding What Goes In and What Stays Out

Let's start with what you leave out of your résumé. Don't mention your age or marital status, and don't talk about your hobbies, your church affiliation, the Harvey Beeker penmanship award you won in eighth grade, or the fact that you play the saxophone—unless, of course, you want a job as a sax player or think it might score you some points toward being named a hot shot young White House adviser.

In my experience, too many résumés read like glacial flows. They contain lots of extraneous information picked up and incorporated over time as the person has moved from job to job but that have less and less significance as he moves forward.

In addition, don't list references. Don't even say that references "are available on request." Instead, save that line for an additional professional accomplishment or two. Believe me, it's assumed that somebody out there (besides your mother) will say good things about your work habits. And if no one will, well, you're in real trouble!

So what does go in your résumé? For starters, if you can, state your career goals in a well-worded *Objective Statement* at the top of your résumé. Résumés are intended to get you in the door for interviews, and employers want to know that you have goals. Stating that you are "seeking a mid-level position in finance that utilizes proven skills in quantitative analysis, spreadsheets, and market research" provides the reader of your résumé with a clear picture and strong "handles" on the kinds of things you're interested in and talented at doing.

It won't always be possible for you to state your job objective clearly. If you're "in transition" you may be looking at a wide range of job and career options, so leading off your résumé with a *Professional Profile* or *Summary of Qualifications* statement makes more sense. This statement is a kind of "capstone" description that a reader can easily take in with a glance and that effectively captures the essence of who and what you are professionally.

What does one of these statements look like? When asked this question, career counselor Mike DeBruhl is fond of noting what everybody's favorite super hero, Superman, might well write down as his Professional Profile statement were he ever asked for one. Mike says it would read something like this:

> Man of steel with a proven track record of success in saving cities, rescuing people in trouble, and leaping tall buildings in a single bound. Particular expertise in: deflecting speeding bullets, stopping runaway trains, and keeping airplanes from crashing into mountains.

Notice the strong use of verbs. Your profile statement, of course, will probably look a little different, but the format can be similar. Perhaps it might read something like this:

> Proven sales professional with a consistent record of sales and marketing accomplishments in the chemical and pharmaceutical industries over a fifteen-year period. Acknowledged ability to manage accounts, develop new business, close significant sales, and meet or exceed sales quotas on a regular basis.

Or this:

> Seasoned association executive with more than twenty years of experience in leading small and mid-size organizations. Particular skills in the areas of organizational leadership, team building, financial management, non-dues–related revenue generation, and membership development.

If you craft a strong and effective *Profile* statement as the lead item on your résumé, you can then tailor your *Objective* to the jobs you're applying for and spell it out in the cover letters you send to prospective information contacts and employers.

Next, comes the heart of your résumé—your *Accomplishments*. Remember the "moments of glory" exercise you did in Chapter 3? Of course, you saved your scribbling from that exercise in a safe place. Now it's time to pull it out and polish the bullet statements you crafted then into finished phrases that can be incorporated into your résumé as examples of professional accomplishments.

In the accomplishments section of your résumé, you want to bullet briefly the key things you've done in previous jobs. Use strong action verbs—"vivid verbs," as my eighth-grade English teacher, Mrs. Duff, used to call them. Also, try to quantify your accomplishments if you can; employers love to see numbers on résumés.

If you use a chronological résumé (appropriate if you're looking for a job in the same or a similar line of work), you'll talk about your achievements in the context of past jobs you've held. (*Hint:* You don't have to chronicle things further back than about twelve years or so.)

If you've decided to switch gears and change careers, put together a résumé in a functional format. You'll talk about the same accomplishments in most cases, but you'll organize them by functional heading (e.g., sales/marketing, management, software development), rather than linking them to specific past jobs.

There are literally countless category headings or "headers" you can use to categorize the kinds of professional accomplishments you've been responsible for in your professional life. They will vary, depending on the nature of your work, profession, or industry, but here are some typical ones you can use in a functional résumé:

- Training and development
- Data processing
- Technical writing
- Customer service
- Sales/marketing
- Market research
- Order processing
- Quality control
- Budget analysis/cost control
- Membership development
- Events coordination
- External affairs
- Meetings planning
- Inventory tracking
- Advocacy
- Supervision
- Desktop publishing
- Software reuse
- Team building
- Project management
- Quality management
- Administration
- Account management
- Leadership
- Staff development
- Strategic planning
- Legal affairs
- Donor development
- Communications
- Legal oversight
- Public relations
- Fund raising
- Management
- Systems analysis
- Publications

As you prepare your *Accomplishments* section, imagine yourself crafting "headlines" about yourself, memorable news nuggets that you want readers of your résumé to remember.

We live in a society where people are reading less and less. For that reason, concentrate on preparing accomplishment statements that read like those that follow. Notice the tight journalistic style in each case and the use of action verbs and active voice.

- Served as consulting editor for a professional newsletter with a national readership. Produced 150 articles in a twelve-month period. Recruited contributing writers and edited articles.
- Frequently invited to be guest on radio and TV interview programs to discuss topics relating to regulation of the computer industry.
- Taught elementary grades (2, 3, 4, and 6) and secondary grades (grade 7) for thirteen years. Consistently rated as outstanding in annual performance reviews in three different schools.
- Responsible for administering the office of a U.S. senator. Specific responsibilities included hiring office staff, developing and administering the office budget, managing the senator's appoint-

ment schedule, ensuring prompt attention to constituent concerns, and supervising legislative research efforts.

Why is it so important to prepare accomplishment statements that have punch? As Bob Johnson, career search consultant with Executrack, Inc., in Atlanta, puts it: "Employers want to see evidence of things you've done in past jobs that successfully got the ox out of the ditch." In other words, they want to see concrete, quantified examples of things you've done in past jobs that made a difference to your employer, to the efficiency of the operation, to productivity, or to profitability.

Normally the last thing that goes on your résumé is your *Educational Background* and any special training you've received. For instance, in addition to your education, you might note the fact that you took numerous computer applications and software-development courses sponsored by your company or that you attended a week-long public-policy course at the John F. Kennedy School of Government at Harvard.

If you've attended prestigious schools, you might want to put your education at the beginning of your résumé, after your professional profile statement. Normally, however, I don't recommend this except for recent college grads or graduate students.

Eliminating the Jargon

If you've been with a single employer for a long period of time or if you work in a highly technical field or for a large company or government bureaucracy, you may need some help in translating your accomplishments into language that people outside your organization will understand. A lot of people who have been entrenched in their job for long periods of time tend to speak, think, and write in a kind of professional shorthand that people outside their field can't understand. It goes by a variety of names: bureaucratese, corporatese, computer-speak, techspeak, even Klingonese!

Salespeople, for instance, talk about "leveraging sales opportunities" and "partnering with clients." Human resources consultants talk about conducting "interventions" with companies in trouble. Journalists talk about "working stories," and people who work in data processing and telecommunications often talk about "interfacing" with all kinds of people and departments to ensure "connectivity."

If your résumé is larded with a lot of jargon, it can be the kiss of death to a job search—especially if you want anybody outside your industry or specialty area to read it!

People in virtually every profession fall prey to using too much jargon. In writing up your accomplishment statements, one reality test you can do is to show your accomplishments to somebody outside your field whose judgement you trust and who is frank enough to tell you, "Fred, this doesn't make any sense. What are you trying to say you did here?"

Another thing you can do is simply to use the KISS (Keep it Simple, Sherlock) principle, as I used to do when I was a television newswriter. To ensure that the average television viewer understood the newscasts I wrote, I always tried to write news stories at a tenth-grade level. Indeed, it was a requirement of the job that I do this!

You might do well to do the same with your résumé. You don't score any points in a job search for being obscure and abstruse. Ask yourself if the average adult with a tenth-grade education could understand what you résumé says. If you do this, chances are you'll keep the jargon and acronyms in your résumé to a minimum!

One question I frequently get from job seekers and career changers is how to handle the question of job titles on résumés. If you've always been in sales, accounting, or data processing and you intend to stay in the same area, fine. Call yourself an account executive, saleswoman, accountant, or data-processing manager on your résumé.

In other cases, however, it doesn't make sense to emphasize job titles you've had in the past.* I'm not suggesting you inflate your function (you shouldn't). Still, there are times to couch things in terms that an outside audience of prospective employers will understand.

For instance, some years ago I worked with a man who was leaving a long-time career with a large company. On his résumé he'd listed his last job as "interdepartmental interface responsible for matrix management activities in the Eastern Region." What on earth is an interdepartmental interface? What the devil is meant by "matrix management" activities in this case? Finally, Eastern Region of what? Besides being too long-winded, this job title raised too many questions. I told him to just call himself a manager—which he was.

Finally, there are some job titles that you never mention. Years ago I worked with a guy who had once worked as a chicken eviscerator. He gutted chickens for a living. Better to keep that job title to yourself and

---

*Job titles, in fact, are often quite useless and fail to describe either your skills or function. Years ago, in one of my first jobs, I had the title of "supervisor" in my company. I used to chuckle to myself that my title was "supervisor" because I didn't supervise anybody. It was a nonsensical job title given me for rating and ranking purposes but that was neither functional nor descriptive of what I did. So, I put "First-level manager" on my résumé, which was more descriptive, easier for people to understand, and also accurate.

just put "food handler" on your résumé. You can use an interview to describe in detail what you did.

What kinds of job titles should you use? Take the common-sense test. Is it a title and/or job function that most people in your industry understand? Then use it if you're continuing in that field. In other cases, opt for something more generic, especially if you want people outside your field to read your résumé.

INSTEAD OF SAYING:	JUST SAY:
Interdepartmental interface responsible for matrix management activities in the Eastern Region	Manager
Supervisor	First-level manager
Customer service contact	Customer service agent or representative
Subject matter expert	Specialist
Chicken eviscerator	Food handler

When you feel you've produced a decent résumé draft, show it to somebody whose business judgment you trust or to someone who works in the field you want to be in. If you want expert advice, seek out a career adviser or counselor, but don't pay a résumé shop to prepare your résumé. It should be conceived, crafted, and produced with your words and in your professional voice. After all, you're the one who's going to expand on your résumé in information and job interviews (a topic we tackle in Chapter 8).

As you put your résumé together, remember this: You're not writing *War and Peace,* and you're not writing your obituary. The object here isn't to outline or catalogue everything you've ever done—just some highlights. So keep your résumé to two pages—tops.

Do the things I've suggested here, and chances are your résumé will stand out from the competition and help you land critical job interviews, instead of landing itself (as many résumés do) in community landfills or in the personnel department's round file!

Selecting References

Lining up good, solid references to sing your praises to prospective employers is one of the most important things you can do when preparing your résumé. Too often, job seekers and would-be career changers have too casual an attitude about references.

First, line up three or four professional references and two or three personal references you can count on to speak favorably about you to prospective employers. But remember, you're going to give their names to prospective employers only if asked for them.

The people you choose as references should know you well and be able to speak in glowing terms about you. Your professional references don't all have to be past bosses, but try to include at least two past supervisors if you can.

Stay away from people who would blast you if you gave them as a reference. Some people are under the mistaken impression that you should list all your past bosses as references. That's not true, especially if one of your bosses was a real jerk. At least one boss out of my past would blast me if he ever got the chance, so he'll never be one of my references!

You can also give the names of colleagues or upper-level managers you've worked with on special projects or who know you through a professional group or association.

As for personal references, leave Mom, your dog, Cliff, and your plumber off the list, but do include the name of a priest, minister, or rabbi, as well as good friends who may know you through business or your involvement in church or the health club. Personal references are making something of a comeback, so be sure to include them on your reference list.

Next, prime your references. Tell them what you want them to say about you. It's okay, too, to tell people what you don't want them to talk about—such as your previous salary, for example, which is nobody's business but your own.

If it's been a while since you worked for some of your references, you may need to refresh their memory about you. Be sure each of them has a copy of your résumé. You might also want to give each of them a "crib sheet" from which they can talk about you to people who call about you. One of the individuals I worked with last year followed this advice. Besides giving each of his references a copy of his résumé, "Ralph" faxed them a one-page summary of the things he wanted each of them to say about him. He personalized the crib sheets to each of his references and asked them to give the following information: a personal description, relationship to reference, key qualities and strengths, key accomplishments, and overall recommendation.

Preparing a crib sheet for your references is perfectly appropriate to do, and your references will thank you for it, since it makes their job easier.

References often suffer from benign neglect. Don't let this happen! Keep in touch with them as your job search or career transition progresses. Touch base with them by phone each time you give their name as a reference, and by all means let them know when you get a job and thank them for their help! References are among the most important people in your word-of-mouth network.

Getting Your Act Together and Taking It on the Road

In this chapter, we've talked about packaging you for the external job market, should the need arise. Now that you're primed for the chase, your sword sharpened and your loins girded, it's almost time to sally forth into the open job market.

Before you do, however, let's talk a little bit about what awaits you out there. Since it's been a while (in many cases) since you were last in the job market, you should know that things have changed. You need a new roadmap to figure out your way around as you explore options and gather information.

Chapter 7 provides you with an overview and an introduction to the new and emerging world of work in late-twentieth-century America. You'll find thumbnail overviews of many of the new work options in the economy today, along with what you need to know about each of them in order to make informed job and career choices. So, carry on!

HABIT #7

Learn to Generate, Explore, and Play With Job Options

> There is nothing in this world that's worth doing that isn't going to scare you.
>
> —Barbara Sher
> *Wishcraft*

As you know, I believe in options. I think it's important that whatever you do, wherever you do it, you create the potential for yet more options in your life.

We are living in times of enormous business and organizational change, change that will create tremendous opportunities for people in the years ahead. I am convinced, for example, that many new industries and jobs are going to emerge and develop at the "crosswalks" or "interchanges" of the "information superhighway."

As George Everhart, vice president and general manager of Apple USA's personal computer business division, pointed out in *Inc. Magazine's 1994 Guide to Office Technology*:

> In the past forty years, technology has spawned entirely new types of jobs—from computer support specialist to paralegal to air traffic controller to medical technologist. In the year 2000, the question won't be so much "Where are you on the corporate ladder" but "What do you know how to do?" And what people earn won't be so much a factor of title or tenure as it will be the market value of individual knowledge and skills.

Technology is also making it increasingly easy for people to work from home, from their cars, or from a mountaintop in Tibet. Witness the busy business executive and editor of a technology newsletter who went on vacation to Denver, trooped up into the Rockies, and transmitted data back to his office in New York, thanks to portable office technology that enabled him to carry a pocket computer, a cellular phone, a pager, and a radio-equipped modem with him in a knapsack. Consider, as well, the emerging phenomenon of "lone eagles," knowledge workers who can live anywhere and who are linked to their business clients by computers and modems, as well as by phones, fax machines, and airline tickets.[1]

There are 9 million lone eagles in the United States today, according to *Inc.* magazine. They include consultants, independent brokers, manufacturers' representatives, financial advisers, writers, analysts, and other free-lance professionals.[2]

What's it going to be for you? As you consider your own career goals, how might you refashion your definition of work and career? Since the nature, notion, and structure of work are rapidly changing, I suggest you open yourself up to considering all kinds of potential employment arrangements.

Starting Your Own Business

There's no question that in today's economy starting your own business is an option that more and more people are selecting.

Many small-business owners work from home, which can be a lot of fun. Take it from somebody who's done it. The commute is easy. You don't have to dress to go to the office, and you can opt for a better brand of coffee than is normally available in most office lunchrooms.

The downsides of working from home are these: It takes discipline to go to work each day when you're just going to the spare bedroom or to the basement; it can be scary because you have to generate business for yourself (what one of my friends is fond of calling the business "anti-gravity" act); and it can be lonely without coworkers to kibbitz with around the coffee pot.

If you're thinking of starting a home-based business, you'll need to set aside part of your house or apartment as an office. And I don't mean

---

1. "Lone Eagles Soar in the New Economy," *Points West Chronicle,* Center for The New West, Winter 1992–1993, p. 4.
2. Ibid.

the dining room table or the desk in your bedroom. Take it from me—if you don't do this, your business will suffer, because psychologically you won't be taking it very seriously.

Second, be prepared for hard work. You'll have to think about getting business by making sales, either in person or over the phone. And what are you going to sell, anyway? Do you want to sell products (e.g., pipe fittings or water coolers), or are you more interested in selling services? You also need to think about advertising, promotional activities, and long-term business goals.

Start now to keep track of your business receipts and get yourself a good accountant or bookkeeper. Small-business owners are regulated to death, and you'll need to account for all your business expenses at the end of the year for tax purposes.

If you're interested in the idea of working from home, I suggest you get a copy of *Inc.* magazine's video "How to Really Start Your Own Business." It covers many of the essentials of starting a business, including: what makes a successful entrepreneur; how to bring a product to market; how to do competitive research; how to structure your business; how to find good people to work with; whether to seek out a business partner; understanding cash flow; finding sources of start-up capital; and how to develop a sound business plan.

Tax Implications of Operating a Home-Based Business

If you're one of the 12 million Americans who does operate a business out of the house, here are some things to keep in mind if you want to continue to write off the expenses associated with your home-based office.

First, make sure your office actually serves as a place of business where you do work for clients and/or meet with customers. The only way to take full advantage of IRS write-offs in running a home-based business is if your office serves as your most important place of business. Try to spend at least 50 percent of your time there, and keep written records of the hours. For some self-employed people—writers and home-based business consultants, for example—this will be less of a headache than it will be for other self-employed people, such as those who spend large amounts of their work day out of the house calling on customers.

Second, do everything you can to strengthen your status as an independent contractor. Nowadays, the IRS is cracking down on people who call themselves independent contractors (small-business owners/

sole proprietors) but who function more like home-based employees of the companies or clients they work for.

To strengthen your status as an independent contractor, get yourself as many clients or customers as you can. Try to avoid working for just a single client, company, or organization. The more clients you have, the more you fit the designation of an independent contractor, somebody who might very reasonably operate a business out of her house.

Third, set up your office in a dedicated part of your home, separate from your personal living space, and invest in your own office equipment such as a computer, fax, and answering machine. As an independent contractor, you may be able to deduct up to $10,000 a year for such equipment used exclusively for business.

Next, consider getting a written contract for every job you undertake, and have your accountant check out the details of the contract to make sure it will pass muster with IRS guidelines. For instance, you might want to designate in the contract that you will be paid in lump sums—maybe 50 percent at the start of a job and 50 percent on completion—rather than on a daily or weekly basis for the work you do.

Finally, get a copy of IRS publication 926, which outlines the twenty factors the IRS uses to determine whether a person is an employee or an independent contractor. Using this checklist will help you structure your home-based business so that you are in compliance with IRS guidelines and can claim the maximum write-offs. Generally, the more "independent" you are as a self-employed person (with regard to the work you do, the hours you keep, and the control you exercise in doing your work), the easier it is to take full advantage of the tax deductions allowed by law.

Is Starting a Business Right for You?

Whether your goal is to work out of your house or to establish yourself in an office, you need to ask yourself if you've got what it takes to succeed in business for yourself. In essence, do you have "the right stuff" to start an organic bakery, produce a newsletter on wine, start up a commuter bus service, or open up a gift shop that sells rare and exquisite oriental artifacts?

As any entrepreneur will tell you, starting a business is one of the most satisfying and rewarding things anybody can undertake. But before you think of getting yourself on the cover of *Fortune*, let's take a look at some cold, hard facts.

The Small Business Administration says that of the hundreds of thousands of new businesses that start up this year, half won't be around two years from now, and as many as half of those won't be around five years from now. That's a whopping failure rate over a five-year period and far from being a sure-fire recipe for becoming rich and famous—or even planning for a comfortable retirement.

Still, despite the odds, lots of people start up their own businesses all the time. If being an entrepreneur appeals to you, ask yourself these questions:

- *How's your health?* Starting a business from scratch takes a lot of physical stamina and psychological heartiness. It means early mornings and late evenings burning the midnight oil, either to write client proposals or get invoices out the door to customers.
- *Have you ever been fired from a job?* Believe it or not, if you've been fired from a job it can be an indicator that you're better off being in business for yourself. Many entrepreneurs report that they made lousy employees when they worked for other people.
- *Do you need to be in control of things?* Most entrepreneurs feel a strong need to control their professional destiny, and they prize independence over practically all else—including a big salary!
- *Do you believe in yourself and your ideas?* Better say yes to this one. Most multimillion-dollar corporations today started from nothing because some pesky entrepreneur somewhere believed in an idea that nobody else would.
- *How much self-discipline do you have?* Entrepreneurs say that what helps them succeed in business is a never-ending sense of urgency—to get their product to market, make sales, and grow the business into a profit maker.
- *Finally, how much of a risk taker are you?* If you're going to be an entrepreneur, you've got to be willing to take risks. If you're not into risk taking, better keep working for the bureaucracy, if you can, and while away your vacations dreaming about the interest that your 401k plan is earning.

If you answered yes to most of the above questions, you may have what it takes to launch a small business. For more information on starting a business, contact the Small Business Administration office in your community, or check out the Small Business Development Centers in your state. They can provide you with information, resources, and publications about how to get started.

Finally, get a copy of *Growing a Business* by Paul Hawken and *Making It on Your Own* by Drs. Norman Feingold and Leonard Perlman.

Becoming a Consultant in Today's Job Market

Let's talk now about the whole world of consulting, which is really a specific kind of small business that differs appreciably from a business that sells widgets or tire irons nationwide.

I work with a lot of people who are going through job and career changes and who want to explore consulting as a professional option. They figure that they can easily parlay ten, fifteen, or twenty years of work experience in their field into a big consultant contract or two that will make them wealthy and independent in no time flat.

After the Gulf War, General Norman Schwarzkopf could have pretty much named his price if he'd gone to work as a consultant in the defense industry—but for most people entering the consulting world, things don't work quite that way.

To be a successful consultant you usually need to have four things: contacts, a highly specialized or unusual field of expertise, an ability to market yourself effectively, and time to develop a business clientele.

Consulting requires hard work and hustle. Sixty- and seventy-hour work weeks are not uncommon the first few years you're in business. And keep in mind that working as a consultant requires start-up money both to live on and to set up an office.

Don't seriously consider consulting unless you've done some detective work to see if there is a market for your services and to secure some clients who can be your "bread and butter" contracts the first year or so you're in business.

Network with professional colleagues to determine your marketability as a consultant. You'll need some regular, reliable clients while you get your business launched, make a few mistakes, lose some business, charge too little for your services (this almost always happens to the first-time consultant), and learn some other key lessons about consulting—like the risk of producing work "on spec" that a client then decides not to buy.

I also suggest you spend time talking to other consultants to get a feel for the flow of their workday and their quality of life. Some people thrive on consulting; other people hate it.

One consultant I know once told me that for the first three years he was in business, he felt like the guy with the poles and plates on the "Ed Sullivan Show." "I knew I had to keep a lot of stuff up in the air all the time, or everything would come crashing down on top of me," he says. And it's true!

Managing your time and allocating your resources and priorities are two of the biggest challenges in starting and running a business.

"Joe" is a successful professional who recalls how, to keep his sanity, he eventually had to move his office out of his house to a downtown location, since he would otherwise work on client projects at all hours:

> One thing I learned about myself early on is that I would give too much to a job. That was one reason for getting an office out of the house, because when I was working at home it was too easy to get up at three o'clock in the morning and go into the next room, which was my office and work all night long. I'm not going to get up at that hour and hop in the car and drive downtown.

If you work hard and are systematic and client-oriented, being a consultant can pay off. People who provide professional services usually develop long-term business through referrals, and if you satisfy your first clients, it can lead to repeat and increased business and demand for your services over time.

Buying and Managing a Franchise

Ever thought of chucking your corporate job and opening up your own Baskin-Robbins, Burger King, or Subway Shop?

As more and more large corporations downsize in today's soft economy, franchises are becoming an increasingly popular way for many Americans to go into business for themselves and become their own boss.

You can instantly pick out franchise businesses with household names: McDonald's, Burger King, PIP Printing, and Jiffy Lube, to name just a few. The allure is strong. Owning a franchise means running a business with lots of name recognition.

Franchises are also popular because there's less risk involved than with other types of small businesses. When you open a franchise, you're not going it alone. You're backed up with support and experience from the parent company.

Here's how it works. For an initial franchise fee, a franchise company, like McDonald's or PIP Printing, helps you get established in a community. They help you find a location and design and set up your store; they then train you and your staff on how to run the business and supply you with materials (for a fee, of course).

Everything is based on a formula approach. The downside is that sometimes you are very closely tied to your franchising company, whether you want to be or not. They often require that you buy only their products and supplies and abide by their rules and regulations.

What's more, buying a franchise can be expensive. Try a quarter of a million dollars or more for a McDonald's. Some are less, of course. You can buy a "Mailboxes, Etc." franchise for $5,000 to $10,000. Besides the initial fee, as a franchise owner you have to pay royalties each month, usually 5 to 15 percent of sales.

If you're really interested in buying a franchise, you'll have to qualify in the eyes of the franchiser. Typically, a franchising company wants to look at your net worth, the amount of management experience you have, and your personality (to see if you fit with the parent company's corporate culture).

If you'd like more information on franchises, contact the International Franchise Association in Washington, D.C., and get a copy of its book, *The 21 Most Commonly Asked Questions About Franchising*. Also, stop in and chat with some franchise owners near you. They'll usually give you an honest view of what owning a franchise is all about.

Working for a Start-Up Company

As more people are laid off from large companies, an increasing number of executives and professionals are opting for jobs in small to mid-size "start-up" companies.

Many start-ups are born out of market opportunity and their ability to fill a specific market niche. They are popping up in many areas, including health care, consulting, training and development, import-export, and in various fields related to defense conversion.

Start-up companies often thrive in tough economic times, but beware: Working for a company just getting off the ground is a far, far cry from working for AT&T, GM, GE, or IBM.

For one thing, there's no bureaucracy in small companies, just details and shirtsleeves. So if most of your recent management experience has involved delegating tasks to legions of staff people who work for you, you won't find this in start-up companies. On any given day you may have to call on new customers, work out the logistics of a marketing campaign, make sure the rent is paid on time, or move office furniture—yes, little details like that.

Which brings me to point two. Small to mid-size companies often get started because some entrepreneur has a new product, process, service, or technology to sell. Often, however, the "idea person" doesn't know how to bring his product to market. So you may be called upon to wear a hat you haven't worn before—that of salesperson! Much of your job may involve developing business contacts and making cold calls on client prospects. If you're not up for this, or if you equate selling with sleazy aluminum siding salesmen, consider doing something else.

Finally, let's talk about compensation. It can be good in a small to mid-size company. But if your primary responsibility is to sell, your end-of-year salary may be pegged to the business you bring in the door. Or you may be asked to invest in the company up-front in an equity arrangement. While being asked if you'd be interested in an equity position with a start-up company is not unusual, be sure to get some independent financial and marketing analysis advice to see how likely it is that any investment you make in the company will pay off for you in the long run.

Whether you work in sales or in a staff or departmental position with a start-up company, insist on an employment contract or Letter of Agreement to protect yourself in case of a layoff or firing. This is very important. Your lawyer can help. Stipulate the terms of your employment, and get your employer to co-sign an agreement with you. Frequently there are few, if any, formal personnel policies on the books in start-up companies. Employment contracts can protect you; if there's a falling-out between you and your employer, or if the firm goes belly-up, you'll be glad that you've stipulated your working terms and arrangements on paper—especially if you need to take legal action to get back pay.

A man I'll call "Gordon" recently went to court to collect back wages owed him. Because his contract did not include all of his job terms, he wasn't able to collect $3,000 that was rightfully his.

Working for a Family-Run Business

Going to work for a family-run business can potentially be a very exciting undertaking. You can often get in on the ground floor of a new business endeavor or the launching of a new product or service to customers. But if you're not a family member in such instances—and even if you are—a word of caution! As the recent Haft family legal melodrama demonstrates, the conflicts and power struggles that can arise within a family-run business (in this case, one that owns Dart Drug stores and Crown Books, among other holdings) have the potential not only to shape the development of the business but to destroy it as well.

Besides having the potential for internal power struggles (succession planning is often a rocky road in family-run businesses), family-run firms can be slow to change when market conditions demand it. Because the business has been formed by a family, tradition and hidebound thinking sometimes abound.

If you are brought into a family-run business to bring more focused efforts or a greater degree of professionalism to a specific department or function—watch out. You may get caught in a squeeze play as the organization struggles to grow in size without losing the essence of what made it unique and successful in the first place. In doing your job, you may have to deal with resistance, suspicion, and even resentment when it comes to the introduction of new ideas and approaches, since these represent a departure "from the way we've always done things around here."

Despite all that, family-run businesses often thrive and succeed and are often quite adaptable and nimble, especially in the very beginning when they are trying to get a toehold in a business market.

The Skalicky family of Alexandria, Virginia, owns and operates a Parcel Plus Mail and Business Services franchise. While Katherine handles marketing for the company, her husband, Jim, handles a lot of the over-the-counter client relations work, and their daughter Kat serves as office manager.

"Running your own business is a lot of fun, and we've certainly learned a lot about each other from having done this together," says Katherine. She adds that at times things can become "pretty intense" when you both work and live with your family. What do the Skalickys advise if you're thinking of starting your own family-run business? Says Jim: "Make sure you have enough money to get it started, because things may take a little longer to get launched than you initially expect."

Finding Interim Employment Opportunities

There was a time when no self-respecting professional would think about working as an executive "temp," but in recent years a growing number of people in job and career transition have gotten on the interim employment bandwagon, and with good reason.

While executive "temp" jobs aren't for everybody, they can be fun and stimulating and, to be sure, a good way to pay the mortgage while you continue to scope out full-time work opportunities. Interim management assignments often offer compensation at or near the salary you were pulling down before, but it is calculated on a daily or monthly basis, depending on the length of the assignment.

Some people like interim executive and management jobs because through them they get exposed to a variety of employers and corporate cultures. Because job assignments are temporary—anywhere from a few weeks to several months or more—they can also be a great way to keep from getting stale in a job or bored with an organization while keeping out of corporate politics.

Hundreds of companies are using executive "temps" to complete high-priority, short-term assignments that were previously handled by legions of full-time employees. Some professionals, in fact, are opting in today's economy to become "permanent" interim employees—because they like the change and the variety that assignments afford.

But while it can be challenging, working as a permanent temp has certain drawbacks.

Typically, interim managers need to be quick studies who can easily get up to speed with the needs of the organizations they go to work for. Indeed, you'll be expected to begin producing from the moment you walk in the door.

While working as an interim professional can be stimulating—you're often involved in handling high-visibility projects on tight time frames—it can be very stressful, especially if your job is to whip an accounting department into shape, implement a technology upgrade in your employer's MIS department, or successfully engineer a big corporate turnaround.

Keep in mind, too, that as an interim executive or manager, you typically have to pay your own health insurance, and there's no such thing as a standard set of employee benefits. You may want to join an association or professional society that gives good group rates for health coverage to its members. And plan to set up a Keough or SEP IRA plan to fund your retirement. You'll likely have to pick up the cost of your own disability insurance, as well.

In essence, working as an interim executive or manager involves all the planning and preparation that would otherwise be required to set up shop as a sole proprietor. In some cases, you may be able to negotiate arrangements for health-care coverage, vacation, and even training, but you will need to negotiate these things.

The kinds of people hired as interim executives and managers range from senior-level executives to functional and departmental managers in operations, accounting, MIS, finance, engineering, administration, and human resources. And they're being hired in a wide variety of industries, from engineering and health care to high-tech and retail.

Want more information about working as an interim executive or manager? Look for the *National Business Employment Weekly*'s 1993 special report, "Interim Executive Jobs," by Perri Capell. It's a great introduction to the whole field of interim employment. At the back of the article is a list of 107 firms that place interim executives and managers.

Also, you might want to contact *Executive Recruiter News* in Fitzwilliam, New Hampshire, which sells an annual directory of interim-placement firms that retails for $15.

Co-Creating a Job With Your Employer

On the face of it, co-creating a job may not seem like a practical alternative for you. After all, you may think, if job opportunities are few and far between and nobody's hiring for opportunities that already exist, who the devil is going to hire me for a job I suggest?

More people than you might think, particularly if you have the right skills, training, and experience and if you can demonstrate ways to solve an employer's problems.

Look at it this way. People hire other people to solve problems for them, not simply to fill job slots on an organization chart. But quite often, employers don't know exactly what kind of person they need to solve a particular problem. Indeed, if pressed, many employers will acknowledge that they don't always know the best way to spot the right candidate for a job.

Second, the best jobs, in this or any economy, often are never advertised and in many cases don't even exist—until and unless the right candidate for the position comes along. (We talk about this more in Chapter 8.)

Given these two realities, why not pitch to a prospective employer ways that you might be able to solve an organizational problem, while at the same time doing things you enjoy and are good at?

This isn't necessarily easy for most people. For one thing, it requires you to be very proactive with people in job interviews. What's more, it requires that you think enough of your own background, skills, and experience to suggest to a prospective employer ways you could be helpful to her that she may not have considered.

How can you tell if you're the kind of person who should consider "co-creating" a job with an employer? Ask yourself these questions:

1. *Do you have unique or unusual skills and experience that a company could benefit from?* Try to quantify or qualify what those benefits might be. What "value-added" things could you bring to an organization that a more typical or standard job candidate could not?

2. *Is there something you've learned to do in another organization, career, or venue that could find a ready application with a new employer?* Earlier, I mentioned how thirty years of acting experience provided Jane Alexander with the perfect background to become chair of the National Endowment for the Arts, although her background could hardly be called standard preparation for the job. Other examples might be the journalist who finds a career in public relations or the auto industry executive who goes to work as head of his industry's trade organization.

3. *How daring are you?* Are you willing to create a new department or function in the organization if you're hired? Starting a new department in an organization can mean headaches like fighting for office space and handling budgets. It can also require you to defend your department's very existence at times.

4. *How much stock do you put in your own ideas, and how willing are you to fight for your point of view within an organization?* Do you have confidence in your ability to leverage your knowledge and past professional experience into a new job, perhaps light-years away from where you were before?

Co-creating a job with your employer isn't possible in some organizations. In very conservative or bureaucratic organizations, for instance, the idea probably won't fly. There are too many traffic cops and gatekeepers to get by. In other cases, it can be worth a try. Last year, for example, I worked with a senior-level banker who, over the course of a number of meetings with representatives of a Chicago bank, was able to co-create a position for himself in this institution. Even though the bank initially expressed no interest in him, he eventually won them over and snagged a job paying him well over six figures. He did it by aggressively and effectively playing up his experience in commercial banking and credit.

If you're interested in co-creating a job with an employer, you might want to consider pitching the idea of a short-term contractual relationship (e.g., six months), during which time you "field-test" the ideas that you and your prospective employer talk about. After that time, sit down and review the situation to see if the relationship is achieving the result that you and your employer first talked about.

Getting a Job in the Nonprofit or Association World

Ever thought about going to work for the American Cemetery Association? How about the National Pasta Association, the American Board of Sexology, the Frozen Food Institute, or the Scientific Apparatus Makers Association?

There are more than twenty-three thousand trade and professional associations in this country, representing everything and everybody you can imagine. They hire people in a wide range of areas, including: membership, marketing, public relations, publications, convention and meeting planning, government affairs and lobbying, and continuing education.

Working for an association is quite different from working in the private sector. For one thing, associations and trade organizations vary widely in size and budget. The American Association of Retired Persons (AARP) has a staff of five hundred people and an annual budget of more than $25 million. By contrast, the North American Deer Farmers Association has a staff of one.

Many associations and professional societies are characterized by a highly individualistic or idiosyncratic leadership style, often embodied in the person of the organization's CEO or executive director. I've seen some nonprofit organizations in which the personality of the executive director or CEO is almost literally imprinted on every communication that goes out the door and on every action that the organization takes. While this can create a great deal of cohesiveness, built on core values that everyone on the staff shares, it can also create situations of micromanagement, tremendous workplace stress, employee turnover, and, in some cases, psychological or emotional abuse of employees.

Associations don't have customers like businesses do. Instead, they serve members or constituent groups. And that's a fundamental difference. One association executive I know says that talking with members on the phone all day (typical in association work) is a little "like getting nibbled to death by ducks"; no one bite is enough to hurt, but do it all day and you may feel like you're getting eaten alive.

How can you determine if working in a trade or professional organization might be for you? Ask yourself these questions:

1. *Do you like to work with people?* In association work you do a lot of this, spending a lot of time in meetings and committee work. Associations and nonprofit groups also tend to be more hierarchical in their organizational structure than much of the private sector, which means that they tend to look for strong team players more than they do "standout" superstars who want to shine on the job. So, if what you really like to do is work independently or all alone, you'll probably go crazy in a workplace environment where many, if not most, things are decided by consensus or by fiats that emanate from the top of the organization.

2. *What's more important to you, money or a mission?* Many people in association work tend to be "values-driven." Salaries, particularly in the nonprofit associations and charities, tend to be lower than in the private sector. So, if you're more inclined toward megabucks than social mission, you'd better think of Wall Street before you think of going to work for a charity or nonprofit.

3. *Like to smile and schmooze?* In a trade or professional association, you'll not only have to spend time dealing with members on the phone, you'll also be expected to go to annual conferences and meetings, spend time with members at receptions, and probably get involved as a staff liaison with at least one professional committee.

4. *What skills do you have that you can transfer from the private sector?* If you have a compelling set of skills in direct marketing, fund raising, or in some kind of administration and management, you may be able to move from the private sector into association or nonprofit work. It helps enormously if you are early into your career, have public stature in your field, or are widely recognized as a subject-matter expert in some area of speciality. Making a career move into association work is perhaps most difficult for mid-level professionals, unless they have strong personal contacts in the association community with whom they can network.

For more information about careers in associations and the nonprofit sector, contact the American Society of Association Executives, 1575 I Street, N.W., Washington, D.C. 20005. Ask for a copy of the *Association Factbook.* You may also want to subscribe to a publication called *CEO Update,* published in Washington, D.C., that regularly lists association jobs that are open nationwide. You can also contact the Greater Washington Society of Association Executives, 1426 21st Street, N.W., Suite 200, Washington, D.C. 20036, (202) 429-9370. GWSAE, like similar organizations in Chicago, New York, Florida, and other states, often conducts job-hunting seminars for people interested in moving into association work. GWSAE also has an extensive directory of individuals within the association world who make themselves available for information interviews with job seekers and people in career transition.

Working Part-Time

Part-time work is yet another option. A lot of job seekers think the only part-time jobs out there involve flipping burgers, but that's simply not the case. In fact, the economy today employs an increasing number of part-timers in many industries. The Department of Labor says 4 million professionals currently work part-time, including attorneys, computer specialists, trainers, and engineers.

And while one part-time job may not be enough to meet your financial needs, why not think of combining two or more opportunities into a single full-time work situation?

Besides adding to your pocketbook, part-time work can you give freedom and flexibility to pursue a number of job or career directions at once. It can, for instance, provide you with the financial footing necessary to establish your own business or consulting practice. It can also be the basis for creating a "composite" career, one that effectively melds, sometimes in synergistic and complementary ways, job and professional responsibilities in two or more arenas—e.g., delivering training programs part-time while also writing a book; working part-time in a law firm and serving part-time as the legal counsel to a nonprofit organization; or working part-time as a high school guidance counselor, while simultaneously working part-time to launch an educational consulting firm that counsels high school seniors on how to get into the college of their choice.

For more information on working part-time, you may want to contact the Association of Part-Time Professionals (APTP) in Falls Church, Virginia. APTP is a national organization that promotes flexible work options for both employers and individuals.

Finding Other Work Options

Still other work options in today's job market include telecommuting and job sharing. Telecommuting, for instance, is being used extensively today by companies like Bell Atlantic, which allows some employees to work from home two or three days a week, while reporting to work on the other days. The federal government is also using telecommuting in some government agencies. If you'd like more information on telecommuting, I suggest you pick up a copy of *The Telecommuter's Handbook*, by Brad Schepp.

HABIT #8

Understand the Power of Other People to Help You Get From Where You Are to Where You Want to Go

> A single conversation across the table with a wise man is worth a month's study of books.
>
> —Chinese Proverb

My first job out of college was as a reporter, first for a radio station in Norfolk, Virginia, then for one in Charlotte, North Carolina.

I loved working in radio. As a general assignment reporter at both these stations, I felt the world was my oyster; my beat was literally "the waterfront." One day I'd cover a speech by the mayor, the next day I'd be dispatched to a hotel to interview a celebrity or to grab a quick quote from a health food guru, environmentalist, political activist, or leader of a local tax revolt.

I once spent an hour chatting with Colonel Harland Sanders about how he'd come up with his famous chicken recipe. I listened to LSD proponent Timothy Leary wax nostalgic about the sixties, reminisced with broadcaster Howard K. Smith about what it was like to moderate the Kennedy-Nixon presidential debates, and kibbitzed with TV game-show host Bob Barker over drinks about how he'd gotten into show business. I even got to interview Miss America, of whom, I must admit now, I asked some pretty obnoxious questions.

Why am I telling you all this? Well, those interviews and the hundreds of others I have done over the years—as a reporter, commentator, magazine columnist, and writer—taught me a great deal, both about myself and other people. I learned how to talk with people. Being able to connect on some personal level with others is one of the most important skills that any of us can develop in business. Indeed, I learned that knowing how to break the ice with people, finesse social exchanges, exhibit grace under social pressure, and make others feel comfortable isn't just social civility—it's essential to professional success.

As we've already said, people are often key to getting critical information that can be helpful to you in your career. With change rampant in our society, the easiest way to stay abreast of what's happening around you and to acquire new information—be it about jobs, trends in your profession or industry, or anything else that's important to you as a professional—is through effective networking.

Is Your Net Working?

Even in the best of times, it's estimated that 60 to 70 percent of all jobs are filled not through newspaper ads or headhunters but through informal connections that people make with other people. In many cases, the best jobs are never advertised and sometimes don't even exist until or unless the right candidate for the job comes along.

For this reason, you simply can't afford *not* to network. You can't afford not to build business relationships and friendships. And you can't afford not to maintain this professional network even when you are happily employed.

Having a good professional network in place is akin to having a good insurance policy in your desk drawer. It becomes a kind of safety net for you in times of professional transition or difficulty and a sounding board and reality check for you at other times.

In my years of counseling people about their careers, I've noticed that a lot of people sequester themselves in their jobs. They bore their way into their organization, climb the corporate or organizational ladder, and achieve a kind of security that feels like success.

But often they do this at the expense of never developing professional friends, contacts, or acquaintances outside the four walls of their organization. This, of course, means that they are unprepared to take advantage of a larger professional network when it comes time to job-hunt.

Even if you feel safe and secure in your job, what if your company should downsize or restructure tomorrow? What if 75 percent of the people you know at work retire or move away? You've just lost the bulk of your professional network in one swoop. I've seen it happen when companies eliminate whole departments or divisions in which there are many long-term employees; rather than job-hunt, many of them simply take early retirement, which can make things tough for the younger employees who don't have that option.

Chances are, if this happens and you haven't cultivated a diverse group of professional contacts outside your office or building, your network will be out on the street! Is there a lesson here? Yes: Avoid professional parochialism!

A lot of professionals tend to get so ensconced in their jobs that they become professionally stale—often without even knowing it. This happens particularly in large corporate settings or in government bureaucracies.

You can't afford to let this happen, either. You can't let your skill-set become outdated or obsolete. Networking can help prevent this from happening by keeping you connected with the world beyond the cloth walls of your cubicle.

The Secret of Effective Networking

One of the things I learned as a reporter is how interesting people can be. Everybody on this earth has a story to tell; if you invest a little time, energy, and curiosity in other people, the rewards for doing so will come back to you in droves. This can be extremely valuable to you in a job hunt or even if you're only trying to position yourself for success in your current organization.

How to "Connect"

Let's start by talking about how to build an effective professional contact network for purposes of a job search. Start by making a list of the people you know: Include neighbors, former bosses, coworkers, relatives, friends, and anybody else with whom you can talk honestly about your career goals. Then go talk to them about your goals, and ask them for advice and for the names of two or three others who could talk with you, as well.

You're not actually hitting any of these people up for work. What you *are* doing is gathering market intelligence about where jobs may exist or could be created.

Even more important, you're continuing to use the "Going Through Focus" Technique™ I discussed in earlier chapters. You are:

- Defining and *refining* your job and career objectives as you talk to people
- Building a network of people, one or more of whom at some point might be able to hire you or refer you to somebody who can
- Gathering the latest information available about your industry, specifically about trends and developments that are likely to affect your employment chances
- Practicing and refining the essential people skills needed to succeed in any job
- Getting to know yourself better as you articulate your personal and professional goals to people
- Getting a grasp on the kinds of skills and experience necessary to make a career change, if that's what your goal is

A lot of people think of this as a hard way to job-shop. They think it's better to airlift hundreds of résumés to corporate personnel offices or to conduct what is sometimes called a "broadcast" campaign by sending a résumé to everyone they've ever met or heard about who might hire somebody someday to do something!

Actually, that's the worst way to job-hunt because it's a shotgun approach that's likely to bring only marginal results—at great time and expense.

Types of Job-Hunting Meetings

There are two kinds of meetings you want to have with people during a job hunt or career transition.

First, there are information-gathering meetings, which help you:

- Research the job market.
- Assess the opportunities that exist for you in a given field, if you're looking to make a career change.
- Strategize and prepare for your next job move, if you're looking to advance in your present profession.
- "Rehearse" your presentation for actual job interviews.
- Get feedback from people you trust and respect about your personal appearance and professional presentation.
- Uncover potential job leads and get referrals to other people.

In informational interviews, you need to be able to:

- "Play reporter" with the people you meet, asking good, penetrating questions designed to elicit specific information.

- Build rapport with people who are in a position to refer and promote you to their own contacts.
- Position yourself in other people's "word-of-mouth" networks.
- Conduct the meeting in about twenty to thirty minutes.
- Keep in touch with the person and conduct appropriate follow-up, as indicated.

The second category, of course, is actual job interviews. In job interviews, you need to be able to:

- Articulate your job and career goals.
- Sell yourself effectively and skillfully answer questions.
- Differentiate yourself from other job seekers out there.
- Look out for "red flags" that may suggest a specific job isn't for you—even if it's offered to you.

Asking Good Questions

In informational interviewing, your intent quite obviously isn't to expose, embarrass, or intimidate people into giving you answers. Instead, you want to build rapport and elicit information from people who are in a position to help you advance your goals. For instance, to start things off, you might ask:

> Can you tell me how somebody with my background with AT&T might be able to use my skills in other telecommunications companies? What thoughts do you have, and what suggestions would you offer?
>
> I'm delighted that Joe put us in touch. He mentioned that you're one of the top fundraisers here in Washington, and, as I am interested in getting into this field, I'd welcome your ideas about how I might do that.
>
> Sue Ellen suggested I talk to you since you are heavily involved in health-care policy. I'd be interested in knowing your views on the biggest issues facing professionals in health care today, particularly as Congress considers health-care reform.
>
> I'm a recent accounting grad, and I'm looking for an entry-level position in accounting and finance that will enable me to use my skills with computers and spreadsheets. What

accounting firms do you know of that might be interested in talking with me?

If you start out by asking broad, open-ended questions like these (questions designed to get your contact to open up), you can follow up with more specific kinds of questions, such as, "I wonder if you could suggest the names of a couple of people that I could talk to?"

Uncovering the Story

With each person you meet in information-gathering sessions, you're "after a story." The person you're meeting with may well have inside information about his industry that can be of use to you. It may never have made the newspapers or been on the evening news, but it could be very valuable. For instance, he might be aware that a new company in your field is coming to town, or he might have a contact in an organization up the street who's in need of somebody with the same set of skills that you have.

Whatever it is, you want to gather information from your contacts that is not readily identifiable from other sources. In many cases, this information can help provide you with back or side doors into jobs.

Presenting Yourself Well in Information-Gathering Meetings

A lot of job seekers throw energy into developing a punchy résumé that speaks to their skills and experience but then fail to prepare remarks to go along with the résumé. During your job hunt, however, you've got to be ready to sell yourself face to face with the people you meet. Sometimes this can be challenging. People will want to know why you're undertaking a job hunt or why you're in career transition. Sometimes they will question your credentials or test your resolve. In other cases, they may inadvertently label or pigeonhole you when you first meet or fail to understand the kinds of opportunities and options you're exploring. Consequently, you will want to enlighten them about all of these things.

I counsel the people I work with to develop "talking points"—crisply worded remarks that highlight your skills and experience. They amplify points you make in your résumé, which you may have sent to the person ahead of the appointment or which you have presented to her at the start of your meeting.

For instance, you might say:

> As you can see from my résumé, I'm a banker with over twenty years of experience in credit and commercial lending. At this time, I'm exploring opportunities with small to mid-size banks here in the Washington, D.C. area. I'd welcome your suggestions about how best to go about that. My strongest skills are in the areas of credit management, administration, and lending.

or

> As a public relations professional, I've been heavily involved in handling media relations and advance work for several U.S. senatorial campaigns. Recently I was involved in the successful reelection of Congresswoman So-and-So from Illinois. At this point, I want to get out of politics and move into public relations or advocacy work with a major PR or lobbying firm here in town. Our mutual friend, Bill, suggested you might have some insight to share, since I learned from him that you made a similar transition yourself some years ago.

or

> As a human resources professional, I've developed and delivered sales training programs for the past fifteen years. At this point I'm interested in finding opportunities that will use my delivery and instructional-design skills to develop other kinds of training programs, specifically in areas such as quality assurance and diversity. What are your thoughts about that?

Talking points provide your contact with specific information about what you're looking for in your next job.

If you're *making a career change,* your talking points should address the reasons you're prepared to make a change and how you see yourself leveraging your experience and skills into a new field.

> I feel strongly that my experience as an executive in the plastics industry makes me an excellent candidate to head the lobbying efforts of my industry's national trade organization in Washington.

If you're looking to *move up in your current career,* your talking points need to communicate crisply the reasons you feel you're a good candidate for a higher-level job.

As you can see from my résumé, I've held progressively more responsible positions in sales for the past ten years. I think my experience makes me an excellent candidate to be a national sales manager for this organization.

"Talking points" help you sell yourself. They're a way to build a compelling case for your employment and to make a good and memorable impression.

After a while, it's likely that some of the information gathering meetings you have with people will begin to generate job interviews. This happens for several reasons:

- An information contact you meet with is highly impressed with you and mentions your name to a friend or colleague who's looking for someone like you for his organization.
- Your contact realizes that she has a need for someone with your unique talents and abilities and begins to ask you detailed questions about your experience and background.
- You make a memorable impression on somebody you meet, and he then becomes a "back-channel" publicist for you, keeping an eye out for job/career opportunities you might be interested in or well suited for.

Succeeding in Job Interviews

Unlike informational interviews, in which you ask most of the questions, in job interviews you get to answer most of the questions.

Which is why, if you sense an information interview is evolving into a job interview, or if you're called back by a key contact for a bona fide job interview or referred to one of your contact's connections for one, you'll want to be ready to switch gears.

What Employees Want to Know

Next to public speaking and death, there's probably nothing that the average human being dreads more than a job interview. In today's tight economy, performing well in job interviews is particularly critical, since there is so much competition.

How can you make sure you present yourself well in interviews? One thing that will lessen the tension a bit is knowing what employers are seeking in a job interview. Generally, they're looking for evidence of four things—your competence (the skills you have); your compatibility (your ability to fit in with the organization); your desire (your interest in doing the job); and your belief in yourself.

Often the very first thing an employer wants to determine is, "Will you fit into the organization?" Assuming the employer has seen your résumé ahead of time and invited you in for an interview, she likely assumes you have certain skills (the first qualification). What she wants to know now is, "Will you be able to work with other people? Will you fit into our corporate or organizational culture?"

Fitting in is a real hot button for many employers, because it's expensive to go through the rehiring process if somebody doesn't work out. Every organization has its own (sometimes odd or idiosyncratic) culture and management style, and employers want to know how well you can blend in.

The second thing employers look for is a sense of your motivation. You may have all the credentials on paper, but are you fired up about coming to work in that organization? Know why it is that you want a specific job and why you want to work with this organization. Be prepared to articulate powerful and compelling reasons why this job is for you and why it's the next logical step in your job or career path.

During the interview, be ready with some career highlights. Throw out a couple of memorable "headlines" about yourself (see Chapters 3 and 6) as the interview begins, and be prepared to elaborate on them later on.

Are you self-confident? On top of everything else, employers look for self-confidence in job seekers. A lot of job seekers are too modest. They downplay their accomplishments. Be sure to rehearse answers to some of the key questions you expect to be asked, especially that all-time interview favorite: "Tell me about yourself." Don't embellish or exaggerate, but don't be a shrinking violet, either. This isn't finishing school. You're trying to get a job!

You also need to prepare for questions about your strengths and weaknesses. On the latter, you don't need to be excessively honest, but acknowledging your human foibles makes you real and much like the rest of us. So confess to the fact that at times you take your work too seriously, find it hard to delegate, work too many hours, or need to take a few more vacations than you do.

Tips on Interview Etiquette

You'd be surprised how many job seekers "flunk" job interviews—not because they aren't good candidates for the position but because they don't dress right, aren't prepared, or don't observe the rules of interview etiquette.

1. Arrive for the interview early enough to go to the men's or ladies' room to check yourself out. The last thing you want to do is arrive for the interview beaded with sweat, having sprinted there from the subway stop two blocks down the street.

2. As you're sitting in the reception area, waiting for the interview to begin, do a little informal sociological research about the company or organization you're interviewing with. What's the decor like in the reception area? Is it nice, or is it tacky? What's the atmosphere in the organization? Are employees racing through the lobby swearing under their breath, talking loudly or screaming at each other? And how about the receptionist? Is he chewing gum and giving everybody attitude? Taking note of little things like this can give you a good sense of how an organization actually functions in real life. These clues provide you with important organizational body language you may want to reflect on after your interview is over.

3. Concentrate on making a pleasant and strong first impression at the interview. Keep in mind that 80 percent of the first impression an interviewer gets of you is visual—and it's formed in the first two minutes of your meeting. So, men, wear a good suit, polished shoes, a silk tie, and a crisply starched white or blue shirt if possible. No pinky rings, please, or handkerchiefs in the suit vest pocket, at least not on the first visit. And no excessive cologne. Ladies, it's probably best to opt for conservative colors—in suits, sweater dresses, or blouse, blazer, and skirt combinations. You can always lighten up later, if the culture seems more relaxed. It's good to add scarves for color, but keep your jewelry to a minimum.

4. Come to the interview prepared. Bring a list of questions, copies of your résumé, a portfolio (if you're an artist, writer, illustrator, or designer), and a leather-bound notepad for taking notes. Stay away from briefcases if possible, particularly big ones. (Big briefcases may give your interviewer the impression you're planning to stay overnight or are going to whip out carpet swatches at any moment!) If you want to take a briefcase to your interview, make it an ultraslim one.

5. Expect the unexpected. Job interviews can be weird creatures. A skillful interviewer will usually put you at ease, while creating an environment in which you feel like being expansive. Be careful! Don't get too relaxed. Remember, the interviewer is looking to get insight into you, so remain professional. Don't become overly familiar, even if

you're generating good chemistry with the interviewer. There will be time later on to forge closer connections.

In some cases, interviewers won't say much to you at the start of an interview or will seem a bit confused about why they're meeting with you. Sometimes this is a calculated effort to throw you off balance or to challenge your resourcefulness in dealing with a pressure situation. In other cases, the person may genuinely not know why she is meeting with you, particularly if the "hand-off" about meeting with you was handled clumsily by somebody else inside the organization. Unfortunately, this happens far more than it should, but you want to be prepared for it so that it doesn't throw you off stride.

To stay grounded and keep cool at the start of the interview, "read" the situation for what it is. First, who are you meeting? Is it somebody from human resources or one of your referrals—a person who may be a decision maker in the organization? Generally speaking, if you meet for interviews with people from personnel or human resources, these are screening interviews designed to gather additional information about you that goes beyond the detail you provided in your résumé. In such cases, the interview is likely going to be a rather predictable, programmed conversation in which the interviewer takes notes and you provide answers. The point in these meetings is not to wow your interviewer as much as it is to pass company muster. It's possible that the person you're meeting with, if not a decision maker, is a decision influencer, so you want to cooperate and provide the information that's requested.

If, on the other hand, you're meeting with one of your referrals, you're going to conduct yourself differently. You'll want to be a bit more collegial, establish rapport, and follow the interviewer's lead in answering questions or pursuing a content-specific conversation about the job you're being considered for.

6. After the interview, always send a thank-you note the same day to the interviewer or interviewers you met with. After someone has taken time to meet with you, it's only common courtesy to send a thank-you note in response.

7. Keep a sense of humor and proportion about everything that happens to you during the interviewing process. In the course of a job search or career transition, you will encounter many people, some of them fine people, professional and courteous. You'll also meet a few jerks who are rude to you or who lack the finesse to know how best to interact with you in delicate or sensitive human situations. In still other cases, people will schedule appointments with you, only to forget to

have their secretary call and reschedule when they are called out of town. You then show up at the office, none the wiser, and the secretary haplessly apologizes for having had you come in that day.

When things like this happen (and as part of the hiring and recruitment process they always do), take them in stride. And don't take them too personally. By all means, don't let them diminish your self-esteem.

Watching Out for Red Flags

Some years ago, a man left a job in a large corporation where he was well regarded and well paid and had lots of latitude to get his job done. He went to work in a much smaller organization for less pay, working for a tyrannical boss who tried to micromanage him every day.

It was a nightmare. As the man once related to me, "I knew after the very first day on the job that I'd made a terrible mistake." This fellow left the organization after eighteen months. In retrospect, he realized that the warning signs about his prospective new job had been there all along. Yet he had chosen to ignore them.

If you're interviewing for jobs right now or if you have one or more offers on the table, here are some key things to consider:

1. *Does the job represent a really good fit with your background, skills, and temperament?* Yes, times may be tough today, and maybe you could use a job right now, but don't idealize any position. If there are aspects of a job you don't like or aren't comfortable with, think seriously about how good a fit the job actually represents.

2. *Does the organization's philosophy and culture match your own?* Some organizations are democratic and team-oriented by nature, whereas others are authoritarian, top-down, or highly dysfunctional. If you are a free spirit, you probably don't want to work for an organization whose leader acts like Saddam Hussein. If you tend to be a self-starter, you're probably going to chafe under all the constraints of a large corporate or organizational bureaucracy.

3. *Is the position you're being considered for a new or existing position?* Newly created jobs can be fun, but they present their own set of challenges. Will you have to fight for a budget in a new department? Will you have to lobby to get a secretary or a staff to assist you in your work? If you're being considered for the start-up of a new department, make sure the job, as discussed, is "do-able" to begin with. Is it, in fact, set up to be successful?

4. *Has the position had lots of turnover?* Lots of turnover may indicate the job isn't set up to be successful or that your boss is such a jerk that all your predecessors have quit in disgust.

5. *Do the position and the organization offer you opportunities for professional growth and advancement?* Be discriminating here. As I've discussed in other chapters, many organizations tend to put people in boxes, and many bosses tend to take the attitude, even today, that they "own" their staffs. You don't want to be so narrowly niched in a job that it precludes you from doing other things in the future. Nor do you want to feel like you're somebody's professional chattel.

6. *Trust your gut.* If there's something about a job that troubles you—even though you've been offered the position—be cautious. In my experience, your gut can be a good guide in helping you decide whether, in the final analysis, a job is for you.

Evaluating the "Fit and Feel" of a Job

Let's look at an example of a job that represents a good fit with a candidate's credentials but a "bad feel" to the person interviewing for the position.

A Good Job Fit

You interview for a job as the marketing director for a small nonprofit organization. You have all the credentials necessary to do the job, including the business and industry experience that your prospective boss told you was important to her in making a hiring decision. After the first interview, you are excited and are asked by the executive director to meet with other members of her staff.

A Bad Job Feel (Same Job)

You hold a series of one-on-one meetings with other people in the organization. In the course of these meetings, you uncover something disturbing. Most of the people you meet with don't impress you as professional. For one thing, interdepartmental politics become readily apparent to you, even after brief twenty-minute meetings with several department heads. Moreover, in these meetings, the people you meet are openly bashing each other. You also discover that three people who held your position in the past all left after just a year on the job.

In two subsequent interviews with the organization's executive director, she appears charming and warm, yet she takes a few potshots of her own at members of her staff. In spite of this, you're smitten with the position ("I can handle any challenge," you say to yourself), and she offers it to you.

Should You Take the Job?

I would counsel no. Even though you fit the objective requirements to do the job, the interpersonal dynamics at play in the organization are not healthy. People are openly disparaging of each other, even to a relative stranger. And while you might discount some of the things that were said to you by members of the organization's staff, it's apparent that your warm and charming boss is, at heart, a control freak who has made each of your predecessors miserable in the job.

The Net Effect of Good Networking

Recently I worked with three senior-level banking executives, all of whom made successful transitions to new jobs in under three months. The average job search can in many cases take longer than this. So what accounted for the success of these three individuals?

First, they all aggressively networked with people they knew in the banking field. These people in turn helped them open doors to still other people both inside and outside banking.

Second, they were all willing to take some risks—move to other cities, go to work in smaller organizations, work in other functional areas of banking, or leverage their experience into different industries and occupations.

Their willingness to do these things was important and not something that comes automatically to a lot of bankers. As one of them confided in me, "I'm a banker; you've got to remember I'm cautious by nature."

Taking risks and being flexible is often key to landing a job today. In the case of these three men, flexibility paid off. One man actually "co-created" a new high-level for position for himself with a bank on which he paid a cold call by aggressively playing up his experience in commercial banking and credit.

The second man decided to broaden his professional background by taking a job of similar seniority but in a slightly different functional area of banking than he'd be in before.

As for the third? Rather than continue in banking, he gave up plush carpet, pinstripes, and starched white oxford shirts in favor of blue jeans, sneakers, and flannel shirts. He went to work for a cause-related nonprofit organization, helping the organization straighten out its accounting and financial tracking systems.

Networking at Holiday Times

Popular job hunting lore would have you believe that it's impossible to make any good professional contacts with people during holiday seasons. But that's just not the case.

Usually, the people who say this are job seekers who don't feel like doing much during the holiday season and who look for reasons to procrastinate.

First, contrary to popular belief, not everybody takes long vacations at holiday time. In fact, many busy executives and professionals like to be in the office around the holidays because things are quiet and they can get a lot done. Consequently, they're likely to be at their desks for a change. And, with the secretary safely on vacation in many cases, chances are good that you can call them up for an appointment, instead of finding them "away from their desk" or "in a meeting."

Second, many people have more (not less) free time on their hands during the holidays. Since a lot of business activities do slow down and people feel less pressure to rush back to the office, it can be a great time to grab one of your key professional contacts for an extended breakfast or lunch.

You probably won't meet your next employer over the holidays. But there's a good chance you will meet somebody who can help you get your professional foot in the door for that next job. It happens more often than you think!

Positioning Yourself to Win the Job-Hunting Game

As a career coach, I am often asked, "How do I know if I'm doing enough in the way of up-front activities to fire up my job search or career exploration efforts? How can I tell if I need to do more or if I should just wait for some of the work I'm doing to bear fruit?"

This is an excellent question. To land a new job or to begin a new career, you must continuously think of yourself as a product that you are interested in selling to one or more prospective buyers.

Figure 8-1. Positioning yourself in the job marketplace.

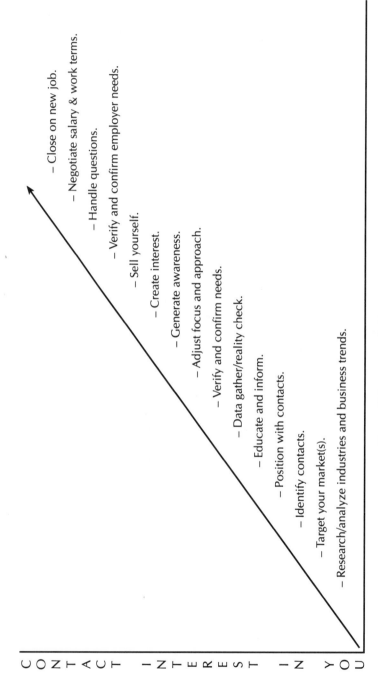

Consequently, put on your marketing cap! Each step you take should be targeted at selling or positioning yourself for success in the job marketplace. In essence, the steps involved in completing a successful job search are not unlike those required to bring any new product to market (see Figure 8-1).

One last thought about networking. Not only is it essential to your career success, it can also be a lot of fun. It can be a journey of discovery. Enjoy it, and it will reap many fruits for you—new friends, professional contacts, and insight about yourself, as well as new professional opportunities.

HABIT #9

When in Doubt, Invent or Reinvent Yourself!

> Don't be afraid to take a big step if one is indicated. You can't cross a chasm in two small steps.
>
> —David Lloyd George

Bradley Pomeroy is a successful, thirty-eight-year-old artist with a versatile palette of talents. In the last few years he's drawn political cartoons for a leading American newspaper, designed collage art that hangs in expensive homes, created award-winning posters, painted haunting landscapes that sell in exclusive antique shops, and sketched memorable portraits of some of the world's great composers for clients such as Time-Life Books.

Now Brad is expanding his business to encompass his newest passion—animal portraiture.

"Artisans have long documented the very special love and appreciation that people have for their animals and a personalized portrait is a very special way to document that love and appreciation," says Bradley, who spends much of his time visiting the homes of his clients taking photographs of their beloved animals, from which he fashions unique and beautiful portraits.

"I love what I do," he says with a mixture of excitement and determination in his voice. Animal portraiture isn't an easy field to break into. Yet Brad is already developing a wide following through exhibitions and enthusiastic word-of-mouth comments from patrons who have bought or exhibited his art.

Leslie Shields is a successful consultant in the Washington, D.C., area. Her most recent professional accomplishment is the co-writing of a book with her sister on what African-American women can do to manage their careers more effectively. *Work Sister Work* has already garnered a lot of media attention and cast Leslie in the role of advocate for African-American women in the workplace.

"I have always had an interest in the career paths of women, particularly in corporate America, and what my sister and I wanted to do in this book was look at some of the barriers that minority women face in their careers," she says.

Part of the reason Shields wrote the book, however, was also personal:

> I've never spent a lot of time in corporate America. I don't like sitting behind a desk too long, and I don't like a nine-to-five work situation. I'm a creative person, and the book gave me an opportunity to step outside and look in at the modern workplace. In writing it, I met a lot of people in every walk of professional life. I love connecting with people. It's one of the things I do very well. At this point in my life I'm not worried about becoming a CEO because this book is giving me the opportunity to do too many other fun things. I'm in demand as the result of writing this book, and that's exciting to me!

Indeed, Leslie and her sister are both enjoying a lot of professional visibility as a result of becoming book authors. *Work Sister Work* has been reviewed by major newspapers, including The *Washington Post*. Leslie has also done a lot of radio talk show interviews. "On these programs we're talking not just about issues for black women in the workplace but also about other issues, such as the relationships between men and women in the workplace and single mothers in the workplace," she notes.

As for her future plans, Leslie has another book in the works. She's also eager to go on the speaking circuit to deliver motivational talks to women in corporate America, many of whom she feels need support, nurturing, and guidance in thinking about their careers.

"I'm doing what I love doing. The money isn't the important thing right now," she says. "Of course, if a million dollars drops down my chimney today I'll find something to do with it."

When he left a job as head of a national organization a few years ago, Don DeBolt didn't know exactly what he would do for a living.

He assumed that he'd find another job in association management, but things didn't quite work out that way.

As he went about the process of actively networking to find other jobs, reconnecting with old business pals and developing new contacts, Don fell into the position of being a broker of information about who was hiring whom and for what in various organizations.

"I had a group of friends, all of whom were sharing information with me," he says. "Because other people knew this or learned about it, I began to get calls from people like myself who were also trying to reconnect with people and secure top-level positions in association management."

DeBolt began writing down the data he was gathering by talking with different people and started mailing it out as a courtesy to people in his network on a regular basis. The more he did this, the more demand there was for "Don's newsletter," and the more his mailing list grew. Soon, people began to talk with him about the idea of producing the newsletter on a regular, formal basis.

"I kept telling people, 'Look, I'm looking for a job. I'm not interested in having a commitment to produce a newsletter,'" he said. Yet interest persisted, until Don had about 150 informal subscribers on his mailing list.

Finally, he came to a crossroads:

> I sat down with a couple of friends of mine and they said, "Look, the association management profession has needed something like this for a long time. We're scared to death that when you find another job in an association, this thing will disappear, and that would be too bad. You've got to turn it into a subscription newsletter so it will survive for the long term."

And that's exactly what DeBolt did.

Today, Don is president of *CEO Update*, a biweekly newsletter that contains authoritative information on executive opportunities with trade associations and other nonprofit organizations across the United States. With hundreds of subscribers nationwide, the publication has become well known in the association world and has thrust Don into the role of career-development guru for association executives in job or career transition. It's a role that the former head of two associations (Menswear

Retailers of America and the National Spa and Pool Institute) never envisioned for himself, but one to which he is readily adjusting.

Moreover, DeBolt has become a big believer in the idea that you can turn a job change or career transition into whatever you want it to be.

"If somebody in the midst of a job search or career change can't find something right away, they ought to invent something to do that will be of value to others," he says. "Perhaps they can contribute their time or work out an exchange of time for services. Doing something like this—that has value and significance attached to it—also has the potential in some cases to make money for you," adds DeBolt, whose asset is now worth roughly a half a million dollars. "You might be able to turn your part-time or volunteer activities into a revenue stream."

Her music delights the ears of millions of country-music fans across the United States, but just a few years ago, Mary Chapin Carpenter was so timid about performing before a live audience that she found it difficult to appear even before small coffee-house crowds in and around suburban Washington, D.C.

Today she has climbed to the top of the country-western music charts, singing about divorce, families, and singlehood. Indeed, she rocketed to stardom with just a single album, "Shooting Straight in the Dark," which went gold (500,000 copies sold) and another album, "Come on Come on," which reached platinum (1 million copies sold.)

At the same time, Carpenter has garnered a shelfful of awards, including two Grammys, the 1992 Academy of Country Music Female Vocalist Award, and the 1993 Country Music Association Female Vocalist Award.

In some ways, Carpenter is an unlikely success story. For one thing, she began recording only in 1987 and had a few false starts with her career. Her first two albums, "Home Town Girl" and "State of the Heart," didn't do that well.

Second, she has successfully pried open the door to a very small and exclusive club of female country music stars that includes Patty Loveless, Pam Tillis, Wynonna Judd, and Trisha Yearwood in a profession that is still largely male-dominated.

What accounts for Mary Chapin's success? No doubt it stems in large part from the thoughtfulness and intelligence of her songs (*USA Weekend* described her as bringing a refreshing female intelligence to country music) and the fact that she's niched herself in country music as a woman without entourage, glitz, or a lot of media hype.

But perhaps the most telling comment about what is at the heart of Carpenter's success is in the lyrics to one of her songs, "The Hard

Way." In that song, she suggests that everybody has two lives—the one she is given and the one she makes for herself.

Making a life for themselves is exactly the choice that Bradley Pomeroy, Leslie Shields, Don DeBolt, and Mary Chapin Carpenter all share. Each has "invented" himself in the work choices he has made. Each has fashioned personal and professional fulfillment for himself not by trying to march to somebody else's drum, not by trying to fill somebody else's job description, but by seizing the day, following a dream, listening to his heart, or, in DeBolt's case, turning circumstances into serendipity.

Seeking That New Pathway—Rewards and Risks

Perhaps you can do the same thing with your career—particularly if you yearn to take the career "road less traveled." Perhaps these people and others like them can provide you with the inspiration and motivation necessary to put wheels or wings beneath your dreams, to do something that you've always wanted to do but have never found the time, energy, or courage to pursue.

At first blush, the idea of inventing a job or profession for yourself that's outside the parameters of most everyday job descriptions may seem a trifle selfish, or a little like wishful thinking. It may even seem immature. The forces of rationality inside your head may tell you that this is no time to think about opening up that hardware store you've always dreamt about or launching that career as a romance novelist.

Yet people who follow their hearts (and sometimes their heads) in choosing a unique line of work often find that a kind of sweet serenity follows them. "If you follow your bliss, you put yourself on a kind of track, which has been there all the while waiting for you, and the life that you ought to be living is the one you are living," the author Joseph Campbell once observed.

How passionate are you about your art or that pet business idea? Are you willing to risk and sacrifice to create or build something from scratch?

If, as you conclude this chapter, you are consumed with questions about how you might proceed in inventing a new career for yourself (one that is off the beaten professional path), I recommend that you simply go out and chat with other people about what you dream of doing. Start with playful and imaginative people who can help you brainstorm and further develop your ideas. Don't worry for the moment about whether the idea is practical or not. That will come later. First, you simply want to give yourself permission to play with an idea.

As you do that, here are some questions to ask yourself:

- If you had your druthers and reality were no constraint at all, what would you do? Be as creative and original as you want.
- How real are the obstacles that may be keeping you from doing this at this point in your life? Be specific.
- Do you have a unique skill or hidden talent that is unused or underutilized in your current job? Could this skill or talent be the basis for launching a business or otherwise venturing out on your own?
- Do you have a hobby that might become the basis of a career? Maybe you have an award-winning recipe for chicken or cookies that could supplant KFC or give Mrs. Fields a run for her money!
- Is there somebody you know who can become a mentor to you as you explore ways to invent a new career for yourself?
- Make a list of people who are potential role models for you in inventing or reinventing yourself. Do you know somebody who's started a unique or novel business or created a job doing something highly unusual or unorthodox?

A Word About Mentors

If you are truly interested in taking a professional path less traveled, it's particularly important that you have a good, strong support network around you to help you do this. I recommend that you first find an emotional mentor, somebody who will provide you with emotional and psychological support for pursuing your dream. This could be almost anybody you know who truly cares about you, who is playful in spirit, and who understands and appreciates how you think.

Second, you need to seek out people who have gone into uncharted territories with their own careers and made successes of themselves. If you want to become a drama critic or test pilot, for example, you need to seek out people who have pursued these careers. If you want to be a wildlife photographer, science fiction writer, or mushroom farmer, you need to seek out people who are successful in these fields. You may think that the people you want to talk with will be inaccessible, but you may be surprised. Some of them may be delighted to meet or talk with you and to share with you their own wisdom and unvarnished advice about what you need to do to succeed. I remember one day when I was in college and thinking of a career as a newspaper columnist. Just for kicks I got on the phone to see if I could reach Art Buchwald at the *Washington Post*. To my surprise, he picked up the phone himself. I then spent about fifteen minutes talking with him about what's involved in becoming a syndicated columnist.

As you proceed with your job search or explore alternative career directions, keep the concept of inventing and reinventing yourself in mind all the time. You may ultimately opt not to take a professional "road less traveled." Still, the concept of inventing yourself may prove useful, particularly if you encounter obstacles or roadblocks on your way to a next job. For example, at critical points during a job search, you may choose to revamp your résumé radically or to repackage yourself to go after job possibilities that emerge from your market research. It will help you to do this if you can think creatively and playfully about your skills and background and find experiences in your past that can serve as pivot points to help you move into a totally different line of work.

HABIT #10

Master the Art of Graceful Change

> Change is not what it used to be. The status quo will no longer be the best way forward. The best way will be less comfortable and less easy, but, no doubt, more interesting—a word we often use to signal an uncertain mix of danger and opportunity.
>
> —Charles Handy
> *The Age of Unreason*

Hanging over my desk at home is a wonderful *New Yorker* cartoon. It shows a busy business executive returning from lunch, only to realize that he's been out of touch with things far longer than he could have ever imagined.

"While you were out:" reads the memo on his desk, "Mongol hordes swept across Asia. Dempsey K.O.'d Firpo. The cow jumped over the moon. Sherman took Atlanta. Vander Meer pitched a no-hitter. Jazz came up the river . . . ."*

Change.

It's become the one certainty in the modern workplace. For all of us. Moreover, the reality of continual workplace change (one author describes the organizational churn taking place in companies today as resembling the permanent "white water" on a river) may very well be causing you tremendous stress at work.

Take "David," for instance. David is a mid-level retail executive who has sixteen years of work experience with a Chicago-based depart-

---

*James Stevenson in *The New Yorker*, October 16, 1978. ©1978 *The New Yorker* Magazine, Inc.

ment store chain. He is anxious about what the future holds, especially since he has weathered numerous waves of organizational downsizing.

"Back in the eighties, I was cocky about my opportunities here," says this father of two.

> I'd just been selected for a plum assignment and thought that no matter what I did with the company I would do just fine—my future was assured. Then, the company began to announce staff reductions and reassignments. Here in the company they euphemistically referred to it as "sending people home." Almost overnight I saw my job disappear from its box on our organization chart. I was able to get another job, but I sweated bullets for a while. Today I have no particular faith that my job will survive in the long run.

Organizational uncertainty isn't the only stress factor weighing on David. He's also working a lot harder at his job than he did a few years ago, since there are fewer bodies to do the company's work. "Back in 1989, there were seven salaried people doing what I do today by myself," he says.

Then there's the case of "Richard," a mechanical engineer who works for a medium-size electronics company just outside Philadelphia. Though his job of the past sixteen years has provided him with an unusual degree of professional job stability, he's nonetheless aware of the amount of change that has taken place in his field just in recent years.

"I decided I had to go back for my master's in electrical engineering when I realized that the candidates I was interviewing for jobs had more skills or more up-to-date skills than I did," he says. "Everything in my industry is moving so fast. You have to have a good working knowledge of the latest hardware design techniques and software, because their application in this business is paramount."

How does Richard cope with all the changes taking place around him? For one thing, he thinks of his job as a constant learning ground. Although he has worked his way into management and away from intimate daily contact with the technical aspects of his field, he has nonetheless tried to keep abreast of new technical developments by reading technical articles. He also networks with coworkers to keep current with the latest technology. "On top of that, I also attend design reviews where there are discussions on new hardware components or design methodologies, so I'm able to leech off my environment to learn what I need to know," he says.

In this respect, Richard is more fortunate than most people. While change is taking place rapidly all around him, he's able to keep somewhat abreast of it and to do things that make him feel as if he's staying current in his industry and career.

Not everybody is so fortunate.

Are You Feeling Out of Control?

Are you feeling stressed out about the changes taking place in your company or organization? You may be anxious about your job security, having seen more than a few of your coworkers disappear each time there's a downsizing. If you're actually out of a job and in the midst of job transition, you may feel as if you have no control over your life.

Whether you've lost your job, are nervous about losing it, or are simply trying to cope and keep up with rapidly changing circumstances at the office, there are things you can do to get a handle on your situation and to stay grounded during difficult and stressful times. To begin with:

1. *Recognize that most people find change difficult to deal with.* Change is anxiety-producing because it trades that which is familiar for outcomes that are at best unclear. As I said earlier, the Chinese symbol for *crisis* is composed in part of the symbols for both *opportunity* and *danger*.

2. *Realize that change is going to be a constant in your work environment for the rest of your professional life.* Consequently, get a handle on how best to manage it in your life. As psychologist Carl Rogers once observed, "The only person who is educated is the one who has learned how to learn . . . and change."

By some estimates, each of us will change careers three or four times in our lives and change jobs ten or twelve times. It's a certainty that in at least two or three of these cases, the change will not be voluntary.

3. *Understand the risks you run if you don't learn how to effectively manage change in your life.* For starters, you may need to get yourself out of denial. A lot of people live their lives on a largely unconscious level. However, the risks of denying reality and resisting change—be it at work or in your personal life—are often costly. Resist change in your personal life, for example, encase yourself in denial of reality, and you can run the risk of losing a relationship you deeply cherish.

By resisting change in your job or in your organization, putting your head in the sand, you risk waking up some day only to realize that your job has been eliminated or taken over by technology, your skills have become insufficient to do the job you were hired to do, your industry is in decline and you haven't thought about how to make a "soft landing" in another one, or you are viewed not as an asset but as a liability or expense item to your organization.

4. *Acknowledge how the change you're dealing with is making you feel.* Any kind of job-related or workplace change generates stress. Moreover, job-related stress can manifest itself in lots of different ways, including irritability, inability to concentrate, generalized anxiety, and a change in sleep or eating patterns. Because so much of our identities is tied up with what we do for a living, the loss of a job, a threatened change in our job or professional status, or the perceived loss of control over some area of our life (e.g., the group of people you manage at work) can affect our self-esteem and mood in myriad ways. Don't beat up on yourself if you feel blue during times of change. Understand where those feelings are coming from. Change always involves some kind of loss, and the experience requires that you give yourself time to adjust.

5. *Become aware of the specific stress factors that may be affecting you at this moment.* Because most people don't feel secure in their jobs nowadays, regardless of their status or past level of performance, they often run a little scared at work, putting in too many hours in an effort to compensate for their feelings of insecurity. As "David" noted, and as studies indicate, people are putting their noses to the grindstone at work more today, largely out of fear that their desks will fly away if they don't.

In her book *The Overworked American*, Juliet Schor makes the amazing observation that the average employed person today is working on average an additional 163 hours, or the equivalent of an extra month, a year. That's on top of an average forty-hour work week. "If present trends continue," she says, "by the end of the century Americans will be spending as much time at their jobs as they did back in the 1920s."

6. *During times of significant personal or professional change, try managing your life just one day at a time.* Take a cue from what people in twelve-step recovery programs often do. People who get into these programs often come out of a sense of desperation. They feel their lives have become unmanageable, that they have no options and no place to turn. By getting together with other people, however, they begin to subscribe to the idea of taking life just one day at a time. Indeed, "chunking life down" this way makes goal setting and day-to-day living a lot more manageable and even enjoyable during periods of transition!

7. *Be aware of the career gremlins that may come out of your closet during times of change.* Because you are a professional who takes pride in your ability both to get a job done and to work well with others, chances are you put a great deal of stock in the idea of being "interpersonally effective" in your dealings with other people, whether bosses, subordinates, customers, or peers. Indeed, you may ascribe much (if not most) of your professional success to this point in your career to your ability to handle interpersonal situations, to finesse or massage difficulties and conflicts among people, and to be a diplomat.

During times of change, however, you're likely to experience moments when you doubt your ability or effectiveness to do anything, especially if you've just lost a job or are dealing with a lot of confusion and uncertainty where you work. This is a common stress reaction to change.

8. *During times of great change, stress, or transition in your life, make it a point to stay in touch with people you trust, whether friends, family members, or professional colleagues.* This is critically important! If you're dealing with a lot of personal or professional change in your life right now, you need the comfort and support of friends with whom you can talk out how you're feeling.

Author Barbara Sher says that in difficult times it's important to acknowledge what she calls the "power of negative thinking"—in other words, the value of allowing yourself to vent pent-up frustration and steam.

"I happen to believe in the efficacy of complaining the way some people believe in the efficacy of prayer," she says. "It's good for you. Complaining, bitching, moaning, kvetching, griping, and carrying on are terrific and constructive things to do. You've just got to learn how to do it right."

Too many of us discount the value and power of feelings and the importance of expressing them. Being stoic and keeping a stiff upper lip seem somehow heroic. They're not. Holding in negative feelings, stuffing them or denying them, is exactly what you don't want to do during times of stress and transition. Why? Because it takes energy to hold all that stuff close to your chest. Venting it frees your personal energy for other things, like goal setting, brainstorming, and creative problem solving. Holding your feelings in also can have adverse health consequences.

Men, take note! In our culture, men still tend to stuff their feelings a lot of the time, rather than express them and process them in a healthy and appropriate way. The risks you run in doing this are many. My father stuffed his feelings all his life. As a consequence, he, like countless other men of his generation, developed ulcers. And they didn't do their families any favor, either.

If you hold your feelings in, you run the risk of releasing or unleashing them in inappropriate ways—for instance, by blowing up at the kids, drinking too much, or inflicting emotional or verbal abuse on others. It's sad, but there are many angry men in our culture—many of whom, as high achievers, don't know how to handle their feelings during times of significant transition.

9. *Realize that being able to reach to others for help and support is in reality a sign of personal strength and health—not of weakness.* During times of job-related stress or tremendous changes at work, you may want to consider seeking out a support group of some kind to help you deal with your feelings. For example, you may want to seek out the resources and services of your company's Employee Assistance Program (EAP). EAPs often focus on helping people deal with job-related stress. In other cases, you may want to seek out a trained counselor or therapist to help you deal with issues of job insecurity, anxiety, or inadequacy— particularly if changes at work (or in your professional circumstances) are creating stress at home or are generating problems with your family, spouse, or partner.

10. *Find innovative ways to learn and to make your job a learning ground.* Perhaps, like "Richard," you're in a position to lessen at least some of the stress you're feeling by finding novel and innovative ways to acquire new knowledge or insight in your work environment, knowledge that can be of value to you in doing your job or doing a future job. (I have more to say about this in Chapter 11.)

11. *If you are trying to manage change at work, don't assume that your employer will give you the straight scoop on what's happening in the organization or on what's going to happen in the future.* Unfortunately, many organizations in transition don't do a very good job of communicating in clear and consistent ways with their employees about what's happening in the organization, a fact highlighted in a recent report by Enter-Change, Inc., an Atlanta-based human resources consulting and outplacement firm.[1]

The report noted that in many cases, those who populate the executive suites in American business today are out of touch with the "people issues" that invariably arise in organizations during times of

---

1. "A Survey of Management Practices During Transition," EnterChange, Atlanta, Ga., 1992.

transition. Because communication and direction from senior management are often unclear, inconsistent, or nonexistent in organizations undergoing change, the employee grapevine frequently takes over. It generates an environment rife with rumor and speculation, where employees are uncertain about what's going on and managers themselves often must operate in a "no-man's land" with little or no direct support or guidance from upper level management.[2]

As a manager within your organization, you may find yourself in this "no-man's land" if you are responsible for managing other people. At the same time, you may face the challenge of managing your own anxieties.

12. *Find ways to be good to yourself, each and every day during times of change.* This means finding time to exercise and to reward or treat yourself for things you accomplish or complete.

Put together a list of the things over which you have control at this moment, as well as the things you don't. Again, borrowing a chapter from what people in twelve-step programs often do, you will find that you gain serenity and peace of mind by identifying the things you're in a position to control right now and letting go of the things you don't. People in recovery programs, in fact, are fond of reciting Reinhold Niebuhr's famous prayer—known in self-help circles as "the serenity prayer": "God, Grant me the serenity to accept the things I cannot change, courage to change the things I can, and wisdom to know the difference."

Even if you don't consider yourself religious, I suggest you adapt this "prayer" to your use. Use it as an affirmation. People in twelve-step programs who feel "spiritual" but not "religious" frequently substitute the phrase "higher power" or some other word for "God." You may want to do this as well.

You may be surprised at how, simply by focusing on the things you have control over right now (as opposed to worrying about the things you don't), you can greatly influence your frame of mind and even your self-esteem during times of change and turmoil. Indeed, it helps you realize that you are in more control of things than you think!

Learning to Ride the Wave of Change

Some time ago I heard a leading business speaker caution an audience of business executives to avoid the trap of simply relying on their

---

2. Ibid.

Figure 10-1. Interchanges on the "information superhighway."

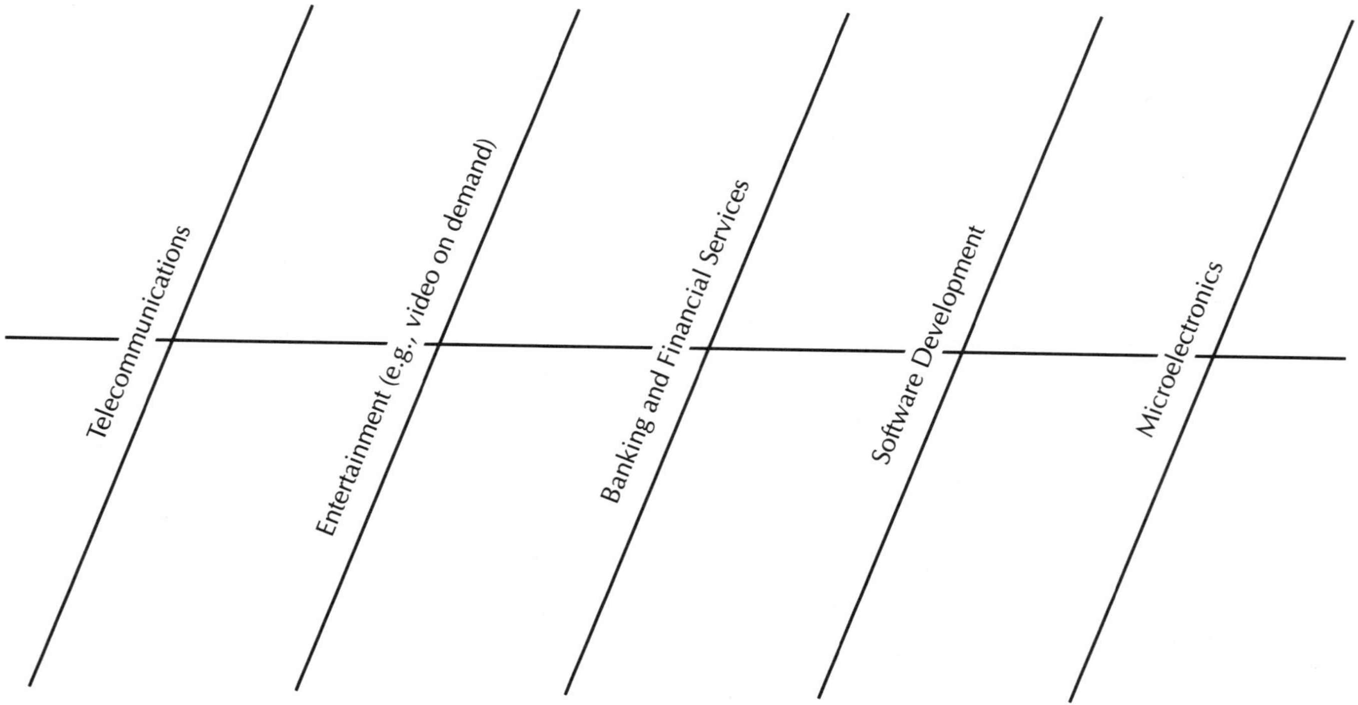

previous professional experience when faced with a new business or professional challenge, problem, or setback. "In times of change," he noted, "your experience can be a terrific ally, but it can also be your worst enemy."

Learning how to deal with change and adapt to new realities is a critical part of keeping your career alive and vital, not only to keeping current and contemporary in your job but to spotting job and career opportunities up ahead as well.

Back in Chapter 7, I wrote that in the years ahead many new industries and technologies are going to develop at the multiple interchanges along the "information superhighway." (See Figure 10-1.)

As the worlds of information movement and management, telecommunications, microelectronics, robotics, and other industries and technologies converge, the results will be marvelous. New jobs and careers will emerge from the synergy of many industries and technologies coming together in new ways.

Indeed, as I write these words, a consortium of companies, including AT&T, IBM, Apple Computer, Citicorp, and a host of others have announced plans to pool their business efforts in order to accelerate the development of new computer and information management technologies, technologies that will provide us with everything from video on demand to a vast list of other online services available via fiber-optic cable hookups to our homes. This is a perfect example of the way in which our economy today is reconfiguring itself and creating new jobs and job opportunities in the process. Another example is the defense industry, which, since the end of the cold war, has begun to shift from the development of new weapons systems to the creation of new products for consumer markets.

Changes such as these bode well for the maze-bright job seeker or person in professional transition who is willing to entertain and explore new options—who is willing to change and adapt! Indeed, opportunities will abound for those who become students of change, who are willing to move away from what have been stable and secure careers and fields to explore new and emerging industries and technologies, leveraging their skills and experience as "the currency of passage" in the process.

HABIT #11

Commit Yourself to Lifelong Learning

> Be not afraid of growing slowly. Be afraid only of standing still.
>
> —Chinese Proverb

How do you like to learn? Are you the kind of person who likes to hole up with a good book? Or do you prefer to listen to books on tape as you take the subway or drive to work? Maybe you learn best by doing or by interacting with other people. Better yet, maybe you learn best by getting on horseback, trotting through the woods, and listening to the sounds of silence.

The reasons to be a lifelong learner should certainly be clear. To remain marketable in today's knowledge-based economy, you need to commit yourself to continuous learning throughout your career—if you want to avoid becoming a professional dinosaur. As a participant in one of my career transition workshops put it: "I don't want to wind up as roadkill on the information superhighway."

Equally important, however, is enjoying *how* you learn. If you love the ways you learn, you will pursue learning with a passion all your life. You will not view learning as work or as education but as pleasure, even as entertainment. Indeed, I'd like you to finish this chapter thinking of learning as recreation!

Back in elementary school, my sixth-grade teacher once told our class, "You come to school to learn, but if there were a way for you to learn on your own, without going to school, you'd learn a lot more than we can teach you."

I've never forgotten that comment. I remembered it as I completed high school, then college, and then graduate school. I remembered it in part because I've always had a love-hate relationship with formal education. I've remembered it as well because I've always believed that each of us has within us an "original genius" that knows how we, as individuals, learn best. When we are infants and youngsters, we're very much in touch with this part of ourselves. It's the kid in us that is intensely curious about people, places, and things. It's the little girl who goes into her mother's closet to try on her high heels and makeup or the boy who spends hours playing video games, learning the programs so well that he eventually figures out how to "cheat" and rack up a higher score than the game's designers had ever imagined possible.

As we grow up and become indoctrinated into the school system, however, we often forget, fall out of touch with, or even disown the spontaneous and childlike part of us that knows how we like to learn and how we learn best. We disdain the idea of having a beginner's mind about most things.

If you had unpleasant experiences as a kid in the classroom, I can appreciate that. I did also. But be careful, lest it affect your interest in and your predisposition to learning new things as an adult.

"Avenues and Venues" of Learning

Start now to think about the ways you do enjoy learning. What learning "avenues and venues," as I like to call them, appeal to you? Which represent a good fit with your personality, interests, and temperament? As an adult, forget about exams. Here, I'm concerned about your finding and identifying ways of learning that you'll want to use all your life. You have a wide variety of learning options and channels to choose from. What's important (in addition to periodic classroom training you may want to pursue for professional development purposes) is that you choose some ways of learning that will keep your brain in a learning and absorbing mode all your working life.

Hi-Tech Options

If you're a computer freak, there are a plethora of new learning tools to explore today—from computer-based training programs that integrate work and learning tasks to interactive video and "hypermedia" technologies that allow for the easy storage, accessing, manipulation, and application of information. Breakthroughs in technology transparency, for example, are making more and more computers "user-friendly."

Although we're not quite to the point where computers can do what the computer aboard the Starship *Enterprise* can do, the day may come!

Not only is computer technology becoming increasingly user-friendly, the sources of information that you can tap into via a computer continue to proliferate.

For example, if you own a PC, modem, and telephone line, you can gain access to literally tens of thousands of external online databases and call up information on virtually anything. You can get financial assistance to help you start a home-based business, pull up (and download) profiles of competitor companies, check the latest fluctuations in the international bond market, or get detailed information on a wide variety of products and services. All through your fingertips!

While there are scores of online information service providers, four in particular stand out: America Online, CompuServe, Prodigy, and Delphi. Services such as these are not only revolutionizing how people learn, gather, and assemble information, they're also changing the way people job-hunt and explore new careers. America Online, for example, has an electronic "career center." You can browse through articles pertinent to your career interests, get professional counseling (private, e-mail, or through bulletin boards), review sample résumés and cover letters, or get information on literally thousands of companies you might want to work for.

In his book *School's Out: Hyper-Learning, The New Technology, and the End of Education,* Lewis Perelman chronicles how we are entering a brave new world in which learning and technology will be intermingled in exciting ways. We will see "machines helping humans to learn [and] humans helping machines to learn," he writes. Moreover, he notes, we will see the great-great-great grandchild of the desktop computer take people where no computer has ever taken them before:

> The evolution of the computer industry has been dominated by the desktop computer—PCs and workstations. The next phase of technology will step beyond number crunching, word processing, and drafting to integrate in digital form on a single platform every medium of information: high resolution full-motion video, high-fidelity multichannel sound, pictures, words, numbers, charts, graphs, whatever.

What will make all this technology so powerful for learning purposes, says Perelman, is that people will be able to *interact* with it. Users will "not merely observe or absorb information, but [will get] unprecedented power to create and act upon it," he writes.

To become familiar with some of the new high-tech learning modalities that exist today, you may want to visit a good university or research library, check out what your company's training and development department offers in the way of computer-assisted or technology-based training, or simply drop by your neighborhood computer store. Taking advantage of this technology may open doors of wonder for you that you never imagined possible. Moreover, it may help you lay the foundation of knowledge for a job or career path that doesn't yet exist.

Low-Tech Alternatives

While computer freaks have a multitude of learning options to choose from today, those of us who consider ourselves "techno-peasants" also have plenty to choose from. Indeed, for many of us, the educational avenues and venues we pick as adults will most probably be not modem- or microchip-driven but decidedly low-tech.

You've perhaps heard those radio ads for *The Wall Street Journal* that feature an upwardly mobile uptown professional effusively exclaiming how important reading the *Journal* has been to his career. Well, don't be too cynical about this sales pitch, because it contains more than a grain of truth. Reading high-quality newspapers and magazines on a regular basis is still one of the best ways to keep abreast of changes and developments in the worlds of business, industry, the arts, and education. You don't have to read the *Journal* necessarily, but try to take in the *Los Angeles Times*, *The New York Times*, the *Washington Post*, or some other major daily paper each day. Also, read at least one of the major business or general-interest magazines each week, such as *Business Week*, *Forbes*, *Fortune*, *Time*, or *Newsweek*. This sounds like pretty commonsense advice, but, unfortunately, we are less and less a nation of readers.

Read publications specific to your field as well, such as *American Banker*, the *Chronicle of Higher Education*, *CFO Magazine*, *Association Management*, or *Training and Development*.

Here's one more thought—a bit offbeat for men, but still on target. I recommend to the job seekers I work with (both men and women) that they read women's magazines, such as *Working Woman*, *New Woman*, and *Redbook*. These magazines often contain good, solid articles and tips on jobs, careers, and stress management at work. To their credit, it is the women's magazines that have most rapidly embraced coverage of job, career, and workplace issues on the holistic level, addressing issues such as self-esteem and how to find meaningful work.

Something else you can do, which I think is extremely valuable, is to read or at least "sip" occasionally from books and magazines that are outside your everyday frame of reference, experience, or interest. For instance, on vacation in the Virgin Islands recently, I read *Think and Grow Rich: A Black Choice* by Dennis Kimbro. I also reread *The Female Advantage* by Sally Helgeson. I was glad to make both these books a part of my reading list, if only because they expanded my zone of awareness about issues, concerns, and areas of interest to African-Americans and to women, which will help me in the career coaching that I do.

Find it hard to carve out time for daily learning? Because time is such a valuable commodity for professionals, why not dedicate your commuting time to reading or to listening to books on tape? My colleague Bob Worley, for example, keeps abreast of the latest trends in the career counseling field by reading one new book a month on the subway. You might even be able to deduct the cost of the books or of your tape player as a business or professional development expense.

Professional Contacts

As much as you might enjoy dialing up a remote database, conversing with others in cyberspace, or holing up with a good book or magazine, there comes a time when even the most ardent introvert needs to step out of his or her shell and get active in her professional community for purposes of professional development.

That's why it's important to go to conferences, monthly luncheons, and seminars out of your office as frequently as you can. This is perhaps the best way to stay in touch with the latest trends, developments, and technologies that are affecting your field and, consequently, the future of your job. You don't want to be the victim of creeping professional parochialism, do you? Then get out of your chair and into your professional community for some fresh air.

While you're at it, you might want to consider taking on a volunteer leadership role with your professional society or association. Not only is this very valuable for networking purposes if you're in job or career transition, it's also a great way to plug in with the heavy hitters in your field. You'll gain important and broadening experience by working or mingling with people from other companies or organizations. Sometimes, wonderful professional friendships flower as a result of these connections. They can also put you in proximity to potential mentors.

As you advance in any field, recognize that a lot of what it takes to be successful professionally frequently involves social activities with others in your profession. That's why it's a good idea to develop the ability to "work a room." If the thought of pressing the flesh for professional development and networking purposes makes your skin crawl, you're not alone. A lot of people hate to do this. But they learn to do it—as you must for the sake of your career. To get comfortable connecting with other professionals in social settings, get involved in Toastmasters, join a community theater group, or do other things that enable you to get experience being "on your feet."

Finding Ways to Make Your Current Job a "Learning Ground"

Don't overlook opportunities—even informal ones—to develop yourself more on the job, even if the training budget has been axed as part of corporate belt tightening.

For example, why not talk with your boss about ways to expand or enrich your job description? Maybe you can get involved in some cross-functional, cross-level, or cross-departmental working groups or task forces, activities that will bring you into more direct contact with people outside your immediate department, division, or work group.

Maybe there are ways that you can make a lateral transfer into another job in the organization, one that would broaden or deepen your professional background in certain ways. Your boss may be willing to loan you to another department or let you engage in an employee exchange of some kind by working for a professional peer of hers.

Why not consider writing an article for a professional magazine or journal to showcase a highly successful project you've been a part of at work? Consider co-writing the article with your boss, "ghost-writing" it for her, or interviewing her for the piece. It might be a great way for you to get published for the first time in your trade or industry press.

Finally, come up with some ways you can get involved in giving presentations either to internal audiences of employees or to customers, company stakeholders, or others. If you've never had the chance to cultivate your skills as a public speaker or presenter, doing things like this is incredibly valuable, even if your first shot at doing it involves delivering programs on workplace safety to guys on a loading dock. Many professionals, even at very senior levels, never develop very good public speaking or presentation skills. Increasingly, however, these are critical skills to possess. They are also among the most portable of skills.

"Stretching" Your Professional Boundaries

Feeling discontented or bored in your job? Chances are you may have outgrown the position you're in but are unsure where to go next, or what to do next. It's a seldom-considered fact of professional life that jobs have life cycles; the things that challenged and interested you in the past may not be able to do so now.

Consequently, it may be important for you to take some risks to stretch yourself, acquire new skills, and be given responsibility for a task for which you aren't completely qualified at the moment. Giving a talk, writing an article, or delivering programs to large audiences of people may seem scary, but learning grounds such as these can be wonderful self-development opportunities. They can provide you with a way to reinvigorate your career, get it back on track, or help you transcend what you had previously believed to be your professional ability and potential.

Leverage Personal Experience for Professional Gain

Perhaps you're dealing with a very difficult or even disastrous professional situation at the moment. I firmly believe that even difficult professional situations or transitions can often provide fodder for personal and professional growth, while paving the way for greater happiness and fulfillment in the future.

For instance, I got my start in career coaching as the result of making a number of painful and inappropriate job choices and career decisions. Although the situations were painful at the time (and aren't mistakes I'd care to repeat), they nonetheless taught me a great deal about myself and what I needed to do to be happier and more fulfilled in work roles. Are there ways you can harvest something beneficial or insightful from a painful or difficult job or career situation?

For instance, women who have been through divorce sometimes decide to go into divorce mediation, the law, or advocacy work as a result of their experiences, because they understand the difficulties that many women experience with the legal system and the impact that a divorce can have on the emotional and financial heart of a family.

Human resources managers who find themselves managing corporate downsizings often find that they develop a "granular" knowledge of the changing nature of managing and motivating others in today's workplace. Consequently, they're well equipped to go into jobs as consultants, organizational change agents, or senior executives of organizations in transition.

There are still other examples of people who have taken personal job/career challenges and adversity and turned them into fruits of flower. Look at Sarah Brady, who became an effective lobbyist on behalf of gun control legislation following the near fatal shooting of her husband, former White House Press Secretary Jim Brady.

Consider the ways in which you have learned important things from times of difficulty. Consider the perspective you developed as a result of the experience, any special knowledge you acquired, skills you learned, or people you came to know.

Realize that a lot of people tend to discount the value of their own experiences, particularly if they can't immediately put a work-related or monetary value to these things. Avoid the temptation to minimize your experiences. They could, in fact, be the springboard to other things, if not right now, then at some point in the future.

Take a Sabbatical From the Routine

While formal education and training is increasingly essential to most careers nowadays, you can also learn simply by developing a strong sense of adventure about the world around you, then going out and spending time in other places. This can be an especially good way to "broaden your professional gauge" early in a career or during times of transition when family and relationship attachments may be minimal.

My favorite example of somebody who did this with his career is ABC anchorman Peter Jennings. Many people don't realize that Peter Jennings first anchored the ABC Evening News when he was in his twenties. But on camera he came across as callow and inexperienced as a journalist.

So, after three years of reading the news, Jennings quit and went on the road to earn his stripes as a working reporter. In their fascinating book, *Anchors: Brokaw, Jennings, Rather and the Evening News,* Robert Goldberg and Gerald Jay Goldberg provide wonderful insight into the making of Jennings as a television reporter. They describe how this man, who never finished college, went about turning his job into a learning ground. Jennings went on the road to cover a wide variety of stories, first in the United States, covering everything from campuses in turmoil to environmental issues, and eventually overseas. At one point he was posted to the Middle East, where he became the first network correspondent on permanent job assignment there. Eventually, Jennings was posted to London and to other cities in Europe before returning to the anchor desk at ABC.

How might you go about getting some further professional education from the informal "school of experience"?

Many professionals find it possible to take sabbaticals from time to time for the purpose of renewing or broadening themselves and/or gaining additional credentials. Professors go to teach at other universities for a semester or two. Artists take time "in residence" at famous concert halls or performing arts centers. Journalists rotate through different job assignments. Even military people experience different tours of duty.

Maybe you could work overseas for a while. As *The Wall Street Journal* observed in a March 15, 1993, article, "Foreign experience, although still frequently seen by up-and-coming employees as a career kiss of death, is rapidly becoming essential" to the career development and advancement of many fast-track professionals.[1]

"Ernie" is an energetic twenty-seven-year-old accountant with one of the country's Big Six consulting firms. He told me that he intended to take a shot at getting an assignment in his company's Moscow, Prague, or London office. "I think it'd be a very broadening experience, and a lot of fun. Moreover, at this point in my career, it's a great way to get my professional ticket punched, since Russia and the former Eastern Bloc are now opening up to American business."

Cultivate a Diverse Universe of Professional Contacts

Although networking might seem on the face of it not to be of any specific educational value to your career, think again. Surrounding yourself with a wide variety of friends, colleagues, and acquaintances is one of the best things you can do to keep yourself current and in touch with what people in other industries and lines of work are doing and thinking every day.

For instance, if you work in a large corporation, become friendly with people who work in small businesses or consulting firms. You'll find it interesting and broadening to know what people in these work settings deal with every day. If you work in academia, don't spend all your time on campus—get out and spend time with businesspeople or with successful entrepreneurs, people accustomed to taking actions on their ideas, not simply thinking about them all the time.

Finally, step out of your comfort zone and get to know people of other races and cultural background or in other life circumstances, like that new Indian family down the street or that single mother of two who lives in the townhouse next to you and who has an interesting job in international finance.

Cultivate such a network of friends and acquaintances, and you'll

---

1. Armanda Bennett, "Path to Top Job Now Twists and Turns," *The Wall Street Journal*, March 15, 1993, p. B1. Reprinted by permission of *The Wall Street Journal*, © 1993 Dow Jones & Company. All rights reserved worldwide.

not only develop a global perspective about the changing nature of work and of different professions, you'll also be well tuned in to diversity and multiculturalism, two significant themes in today's workplace.

Develop a strong sense of curiosity about the world around you. As children, most of us are intensely curious. We ask a lot of questions and are frequently told that doing so is impolite. By the time we get to high school, most of us have internalized this message pretty well, which is why high school and college teachers often have a tough time prying classroom participation out of cynical adolescents.

As adults, a lot of people don't show any particular curiosity about the world around them. In fact, they have what I call a "lousy curiosity quotient," or "LCQ."

Having been a reporter earlier in my career, I'm very much biased in favor of being curious about the world around me and asking questions in order to broaden my knowledge of things. Take notice of the environment and the people around you, because both can provide you with clues about your career and insight about your life. For example, next time you go to a party, find out what at least five other people in the room do for a living. It might make for some very interesting conversation. And you might make some good networking contacts, too!

Develop an Interdisciplinary World View

A lot of people live their lives with blinders on. Because they never step out of the box of their current frame of reference, they never cultivate the presence of mind about living that enables them to take experiences from one realm of their life and apply them in another. Yet, we human beings are uniquely capable of doing this. It is, in fact, the basis of our creativity, ingenuity, and resourcefulness and has been the basis for countless human discoveries, inventions, and advances in everything from medicine and science to technology, healthcare, and human development, not to mention being the source of wealth, fame, and economic success for some.

Thomas Edison once said, "Make it a practice to keep on the lookout for novel and interesting ideas that others have used successfully. Your idea has to be original only in its adaptation to the problem you are working on."

In some ways, Nolan Bushnell is a modern-day Thomas Edison. Bushnell, who founded Atari and created Chuck E. Cheese, is an enthusiastic advocate of interdisciplinary thinking. As he once told *Success* magazine, "At a very early age, I determined that I was always going to stay on the steep part of the learning curve. Many times the act of creation is nothing more than taking something very standard in one business and applying it to another. It helps to have a wide knowledge base. I spent my college days working in an amusement park, so I was able to combine my knowledge of the economics of the amusement field to video technology and computers to found Atari and invent the video game."[2]

Bushnell's commitment to learning—and to interdisciplinary thinking—has paid off handsomely for him. After starting Atari in 1972, he sold it four years later for a cool $28 million!

How might you use a little interdisciplinary thinking to give your career a boost or help you achieve breakthrough financial success?

Take "Mental Health" Breaks

When I need to get out of the office or give myself a "mental health" break, I often go to bookstores and spend an hour or so scouring the bookshelves and browsing through books that catch my eye or excite my interest. I like to call this type of recreational learning "intellectual grazing."

With the growing number of discount bookstore chains in most cities, there are often a lot of places where you can go, browse through bookstore shelves, find a book or two to buy, and then pull up a chair and enjoy a cup of cappuccino as you delve into a self-help book, *People*, or *Parade*. I encourage you to do things like this. Not only are they good diversions from numbing office work and enervating office politics, they can often stimulate your mind to think in new ways about what you want to do with the rest of your life or what you want to do next in your career. Indeed, I often get some of my best ideas for seminars, articles, and radio essays by letting my ideas "cross-pollinate" with things I read, learn about, or just think about while surrounded by the ambience of a bookstore or coffeehouse.

A variation of this approach to learning is to pick up a big stack of magazines when you're going on a business trip and indulge yourself en route to your destination by poring over the latest issues of all the periodicals you subscribe to but never get a chance to read at home. I also like to pick up copies of magazines I don't subscribe to and that are on subjects far afield from my normal activities and interests but that

---

2. Paul Chu and Jason Forsyth, "Brainstorm," *Success*, October 1993, pp. 30–31. Reprinted with permission of *Success* magazine. Copyright © 1993 by Hal Holdings Corporation.

pique my curiosity. In fact, that's how I first discovered *Garbage* and *Success* magazines, which I have come to enjoy a great deal.

When I'm on business trips I also like to take a highlighter with me. As I read things of interest, I highlight key passages and mark pages that I then tear out or copy later for future reference.

You'd be surprised at how easily, when you get out of your everyday routine, you can develop new perspectives on yourself or on problems at work simply by taking quiet time while on a train or plane to hole up with yourself mentally.

Why do "get-away" recreational learning activities such as these work? The brain, I find, is like a fertile field. You need creative pauses in your busy routine from time to time to walk the land of your own mind, turn over fresh earth, plant seeds of personal interest or awareness, and harvest new insights into yourself. Learning like this almost constitutes a minivacation for me!

One of the best ways to nurture your continuing mental health and intellectual growth at work is to give yourself some meaningful downtime at the office each day.

Whether you're a secretary, CEO, florist, statistician, or mortician, you need (and I stress the word *need*) time at work each day when you can put your mind in neutral and your tongue in park. I had a boss who once said she budgeted at least fifteen minutes a day just to "veg out" or look out the window and silently scream to the office dwellers across the plaza—and she allotted twenty minutes a day from January through March, when the diminished amount of sunlight contributed to her getting a mild case of Seasonal Affect Disorder!

Don't underestimate the importance of mental leisure and healthy diversion as a part of your workday. Even the most sophisticated and serious professional needs to give herself the chance to be like a kid at times. Indeed, taking a playful attitude toward things at work can sometimes unclog mental logjams in your head or help you survive difficult workplace circumstances.

Find Meaning in Your Work

Ask yourself whether you find passion in your work right now. This is perhaps the most fundamental career question of all, and it relates enormously to life-long learning.

No job or career is going to feel perfect all the time. Yet, to be sustained by your work, to bring energy to it on a continual basis, you have to get something from it that lights your passion and excites your heart.

Do you get absorbed in your work? Do you have moments when it feels like you're exactly where you're supposed to be?

Psychologist Rollo May once said, "When you are completely absorbed or caught up in something, you become oblivious to things around you, or to the passage of time. It is this absorption in what you are doing that frees your unconscious and releases your creative imagination."

You may be asking, "How do I know if I'm in the right kind of job and career? What if I'm not sure whether there's anything better for me out there?"

Only you and your heart can truly tell if you are in the right field. Let me share with you the examples of two people who have found their calling. One of them is in the priesthood, the other in journalism. Perhaps their reflections will give you something of a benchmark by which to judge your own feelings.

"Joan" is a thirty-three-year-old woman recently ordained to the Episcopal priesthood. It has taken her six years to work her way through the rites of passage required by the institutional church to become a priest. Along the way she's had to battle sexism and the glass ceiling. Yet she feels she's in the right place. As a teenager involved in church work and later as a pastoral intern, she knew that she had found her calling:

> I can't describe it any better than to say that I was at home. I felt a love for the work, a fulfillment serving other people, working with people, preaching, and teaching. I felt my life had meaning. I'm aware that I'm living my life to the fullest, and there is a peace and serenity and an excitement about what I do that I have never found in any other job or career situation.

"John" is a journalist. He too feels he's where he's supposed to be and wants to be.

> As a journalist, you come into contact with people who are shaping history. I have seen presidents a number of times. I've seen two queens. You meet powerful business leaders. Two weeks ago, for instance, I interviewed [Secretary of Labor] Robert Reich. Journalism is one of those fields that frequently calls upon every experience that you have ever had, every book that you have ever read, and every person you have ever met. If you are resourceful, if you are fast, if

you have a good memory, if you are able to make connections, I think this is the most wonderful field in the world.

Have you found your mission? Do you experience passion in your work? If not, why not? Have you lost interest or simply drifted off course from where you really should be going? Your continuing education "assignment" may be to see if you can recapture the passion you felt about your work at an earlier time.

Or perhaps now is the time to explore a new-found interest to see if it might be the basis for a new calling, a new career.

Whatever you decide to do, remember, you deserve to find meaning in your work and to derive satisfaction from its doing. W. E. B. Dubois once wrote, "The return from your work must be the satisfaction which that work brings you. With this, life is heaven, or as near heaven as you can get. Without this—with work which you despise, which bores you, and which the world does not need—this life is hell."

HABIT #12

Cultivate Emotional and Psychological Heartiness

> Happiness, better yet sustainable joy, is gained to the degree we handle whatever life gives us to master. Sometimes this means we must control events, and sometimes this means we must let go of control, renunciating, accepting what is in good faith and simple, uncomplicated dignity. Those who are able to resolve this paradox without requiring a rule for every specific situation are on their way to lasting well-being.
>
> —Marsha Sinetar
> *Living Happily Ever After*

Some time ago, ABC's "20/20" ran a fascinating story on centenarians, the growing population of Americans who are one hundred years old and older.

There are, in fact, thirty-six thousand centenarians in the United States today. In his report, which profiled the lives of a number of these remarkable men and women, reporter Hugh Downs highlighted some of the qualities that people in this age group tend to display. Among other things, centenarians tend to be optimistic, engaged with other people, active and mobile, and able to deal effectively with loss.

All of these qualities contribute to a quality that I like to call "emotional and psychological heartiness." While it's something that successful centenarians undoubtedly possess, it's a quality that I think it behooves people of any age to cultivate in order to get the most out of life and to be healthy, both in body and in outlook.

Certainly, for purposes of planning a successful and happy career, it's important to cultivate qualities of emotional and psychological heartiness in order to navigate effectively the inevitable rough spots that life puts in our paths and to deal with the stress that is inherent in all of life.

While you can't eliminate stress and change from your life and wouldn't want to (the Reverend Norman Vincent Peale once remarked that the only people in this world who don't have any problems are in cemeteries), there are things you can do to develop the emotional and psychological heartiness so necessary to career success and to a high quality of life.

Let's talk about what you can do to tone your body, brighten your spirit, and train yourself to have an optimistic outlook about life. Let's start by getting physical.

Don't Let Yourself Go to Waist

I don't know about you, but as a kid I didn't display a lot of athletic prowess. I was, in fact, the last kid picked for softball games in elementary school and grew up with a massive inferiority complex about my athletic abilities.

But when I went to college, I discovered running.

I went to college at William and Mary, located in scenic Colonial Williamsburg, Virginia, one of this country's tourist meccas. As a sophomore in college, I got into the habit of running each day between the colonial Capitol, located at one end of Duke of Gloucester Street, and the historic Wren Building, located at the other end.

What I noticed each time I finished running was how good I felt and how any negative feelings I may have had at the start of my exercise routine had dissipated by the time I was finished. I later learned that this was due to the endorphins that got pumped into my system as the result of such strenuous, sustained exercise, the like of which I'd never known before in my life!

Today, twenty years later, I still run regularly, combining my "roadwork," as we runners like to say, with workouts on the Stairmaster at my gym. I'm no gym god with chiseled pectorals, nor am I likely to be a candidate for the decathlon anytime soon, but I know this: I'm fit and trim and aware that regular exercise has done wonders for me all these years, improving everything from my muscle tone to my skin tone!

I find, for instance, that when I'm feeling stressed out or depressed, exercise is a great tension reliever. It lifts my spirits. Moreover, regular exercise seems to toughen my sense of self-esteem and my belief in my ability to accomplish the things I want in my life.

If you're not into a regular exercise routine right now, I suggest you get one. See your doctor if you have any questions about your fitness, but then do it! Choose some physical activity that you find enjoyable, because you'll do it consistently only if you enjoy it! If you don't like pushups, don't do them. Personally, I hate pushups, but I love to run, play tennis, and swim. Choose a mix of physical activities that you enjoy and that can help build stamina, physical flexibility, and at least some muscle strength at the same time. Then make it a habit to pursue your exercise routine at least three or four times a week.

Eat Body-Friendly, Heart-Healthy Foods

For the most part, Americans have lousy (to say nothing of lazy) eating habits. We eat too much fat and red meat and not enough fruits, vegetables, and fiber.

Do I sound like an ad for your local health food store? Growing up, I ate hamburgers almost every day, along with processed cheese, potato chips, and a thousand and one other foods that only added inches to my hips. Not anymore!

Some time ago I smartened up to the fact that if I choose carefully the foods I eat, it's not only fairly easy for me to maintain my body weight, I also feel better to boot. For instance, I almost never eat red meat unless I'm out and somebody serves me filet mignon or a barbequed hamburger. In those cases, I relent a bit. But I don't do it too frequently.

Instead, I have discovered fish. My local market carries a wide variety of fish, from salmon and swordfish to more exotic cuts like Chilean sea bass. I may be forty years old, but I love to eat! And I find I can eat a lot (in terms of volume) if I simply pay attention to the fat content of the food I take in. I skip heavy-duty desserts and sauces, for the most part, and steer clear of most processed foods. When I do feel a craving for sweets, I head for the frozen nonfat yogurt case at my local gourmet supermarket. I have discovered a wonderful vanilla fudge frozen yogurt that contains no fat and only 150 calories per serving! Because there's no fat in it at all, I devour this stuff many times each week.

If you don't have a healthy diet, it's high time you started eating smart. It's not that hard to do, and you'll find that it's not only healthy for your body, it improves your thinking processes as well.

Try a Little Healthy Selfishness

Regardless of who you are, and what your family, work, and life circumstances are, it's important that you carve out some time for yourself each day, apart from family obligations, work, a job search, and personal primary relationships. All of us need solitary time to commune with ourselves and to regain the energy and perspective necessary to live lives in balance. Yet this is something a lot of people, particularly high-functioning, driven professionals, fail to do.

What do you enjoy doing for yourself? Maybe you enjoy:

- Taking yourself out for lunch or dinner to a favorite restaurant that only you know about
- Floating through a favorite store or boutique in search of things for the house
- Going to a favorite museum on a rainy day
- Holing up by yourself at home with a good book, a cup of coffee, or a glass of wine

Some people need to pay particular attention to finding time for relaxation, rest, and respite from the hustle and bustle of life. They include:

- Single parents
- Mothers who spend most of their lives taking care of others, whether at work or at home
- Men who tend to work more than they should and who consequently never develop any hobbies or interests apart from work
- Helping professionals (everybody from therapists to school teachers) who tend to focus their energies and attention on others
- Adult children of alcoholics and others from dysfunctional homes where the healthy care of oneself was never acknowledged, recognized, or emphasized

Do you have trouble giving to yourself? Do you feel guilty when you treat yourself well? Surprisingly, a lot of people do. Americans take less annual vacation time than people in practically any other Western country. At the same time, many employers, including many law firms, consulting firms, major corporations, and privately run companies, consider a sixty- to eighty-hour work week normal. "Work addiction" has become the most accepted and encouraged of all the addictions, notes author Bryan Robinson in his book of the same name.

What can you do to ensure that you practice "healthy selfishness" on a regular basis? Here are some ideas:

- Write down the things you enjoy doing by yourself, and then commit yourself to doing those things at least a little bit each week.

- "Contract" with a trusted friend to monitor your progress in giving to yourself. Get together with this person each week, either in person or over the phone, to describe your progress.
- Recognize that if you don't take the initiative to take care of yourself, no one else will. As a friend of mine is fond of saying, "Nobody is ever going to congratulate you for taking a vacation."
- Pay attention to the signals from your body or mind that indicate that you need to slow down, take a break from your routine, or otherwise switch gears. You'll know it's time to take some time for yourself if you feel sluggish or irritable or find it hard to concentrate.
- Take regular vacations for relaxation and renewal. Too many Americans accumulate annual leave and don't take even two weeks of vacation each year. Be good to yourself, and mark vacation off on the calendar right now!

Understand the Power of Friendships

During times of stress and transition, it's important that you tap into the power of friends for support and love. They are essential for cultivating emotional and psychological heartiness. Women tend to forge deeper friendships than many men do, which means they are able to ask for and receive emotional support in many ways that men seldom experience.

If you're a man, you may want to take this occasion in your life to assess the status of your friendships, with other men and with women, and to look at ways that you can deepen friendships with people you care about.

Many men hunger for closer friendships with other men. Unfortunately, our society doesn't do a very good job of helping men reach out to other men for support and companionship.

My dear friend Jack Rodland is one of the people to whom this book is dedicated. I knew Jack for twenty years, and it's fair to say that my life was forever changed by his presence in my life. Jack was the minister of music at my hometown church. He saw me grow from an awkward adolescent, singing baritone in his church choirs, into a man. He helped me through any number of personal crises, including one in which I had to take a year off from college for nervous exhaustion.

All through my college and graduate-school years, Jack was there for me. I am convinced that it is because of the friendship he offered to me, first as a "coach" and teacher and later as a true friend, that I never went off the deep end, never got into drugs or into any other serious kind of trouble. I always had a place where I could go and talk things out with somebody whom I knew cared about me. Jack created a big safe space in our friendship where I could simply and easily be myself.

Several years ago, Jack died of cancer. He was only forty-eight years old and left a wife and two children.

As a friend, Jack offered me unconditional love. That's what the best friendships are all about. And men, you need them every bit as much as women do!

Having a close and loving network of people around you is one of the most important things you can do to help you get through tough times. Don't be modest or let false pride keep you from being able to lean emotionally on others. People may take it as a compliment if you feel safe enough with them to share what you are *really* feeling.

Create a Family of Choice for Yourself

Increasingly, our society is becoming one in which many people are living alone, for all kinds of reasons. It can be very difficult for single people, particularly at holiday and vacation times, if they don't have a biological family to be with. Given the dysfunctional nature of so many families today, it's sometimes not even advisable for people to spend much time with their biological families, *particularly* at holiday time!

For that reason, I encourage you to create a family of choice around you, if this is appropriate. If you're a single or divorced person, a gay or lesbian person without a primary relationship, a handicapped person without close family ties, or a refugee from a dysfunctional family, seek out friends with whom you can create a "family" of choice. In many large cities, churches, synagogues, organized social activities, and twelve-step programs provide the means for creating such modern families by enabling individuals to come together and be together.

Don't be shy about creating or wanting a family of choice for yourself. It may be the healthiest thing in the world for you. You may well find that it gives you the kind of emotional and psychological support that you have yearned for all your life but never received from your biological family.

Find Ways to Serve Other People

A balanced life requires that we find ways to serve other people through our work and with our presence.

I'm a big believer in the idea that there are multiple ways to serve, both in the workplace and in volunteer activities. On a spiritual level, I subscribe to the notion that while we are here on this planet, we are meant to taste both of prosperity and of the poignant disparity that can sometimes keep us apart from others. It is our personal awareness of this disparity, I think, that often fuels the urge to be of service to others, to "bridge the gap," and to help others realize more of life for themselves.

Anyone who has ever rolled up her sleeves to work in a holiday soup kitchen or who has volunteered his time and talents to a cancer campaign knows what I am talking about. When we find ways to help others, our own difficulties and challenges often pale in comparison!

I sometimes tell the individuals I work with to balance their job-search efforts with some kind of service to others. There are times when this results in professional, as well as psychic, payoffs. It's not unheard of, for example, for people in job and career transition to discover new careers for themselves in public service, nonprofit management, or charity work as the result of being involved in volunteer activities. Being a volunteer leader of a nonprofit organization or being involved in volunteer activities can also bring meaning to your life at times when work seems devoid of much meaning and can help you gain a much needed perspective on life. As Albert Schweitzer once observed, "The only ones among you who will be really happy are those who will have sought out and found how to serve."

Don't Take Yourself Too Seriously!

As much as anything else, developing emotional and psychological heartiness involves developing a sense of humor about life, one that enables you to keep from taking yourself too seriously while simultaneously helping you deal with all the curve balls that life sees fit to toss your way.

One thing that's key to developing a good sense of humor is nurturing something of the attitude of an insurrectionist, a fighter who isn't about to let life get the better of him. "A warrior must only take care that his spirit is never broken," remarked Shissai. Use humor to laugh at your circumstances when the only other alternative is to cry.

Cultivate an Attitude of Positive Expectation

Finally, find ways to fill your life with passion, and get excited about the possibilities that life has to offer you. What you feel passionate about may well give you clues about where your heart feels most at home—and, consequently, where you might be able to build a career for yourself. Maybe your passion is spending time with kids, creating beautiful watercolor seascapes, preparing an elegant plate of food for guests, writing short stories, or making people laugh. Ask yourself what really gives your life a lift.

Be extremely honest with yourself. Listen to your heart, as well as your intellect. Too many people make job and career choices not out of a sense of what they want or intuitively know is right for them but out of a sense of duty to what other people want or expect of them or to what society will admire. I believe you must be true to yourself. As Shakespeare said, "To thine own self be true."

Perhaps you feel it's too late for you to make a job or career change, that your life is already determined for you. Is that really true? Or do you simply use it as an excuse for not taking action to improve your life?

Nobody can find your professional identity—your "vocational voice"—for you. But a lot of people can help. In his wonderful little book, *The Alchemist*, author Paulo Coehlo tells the story of an Andalusian shepherd boy who goes in pursuit of his dreams. In the course of his journey, he encounters a shaman who encourages him to keep going, even when dark shadows seem to crowd in on him from all sides, foreshadowing disaster. The man's message to the boy is this: "When you want something, all the universe conspires in helping you to achieve it." And so the boy goes forward in faith, paying attention to what the man refers to as the "good omens" in his life and believing that he will indeed find answers to his questions.

If you are feeling a little lost or have doubts about what you do next with your career, be gentle with yourself, listen to your heart, assess your skills and experience, and talk with people you trust. Cultivate a sense of faith in your own ability to make informed career decisions.

Finally, move forward with your plans, one day at a time. Be open to exploring options and avenues that present themselves to you. But remember: Even the most thorough job search or exploration of alternative careers is going to be loaded with dead leads. And in the course of your journey, my friend, you may find that serendipity plays as large a role as planning and persistence in helping you find your professional destiny.

References and Suggested Reading

Aburdene, Patricia, and John Naisbitt. *Megatrends for Women.* New York: Fawcett Columbine, 1992.
Bennett, Amanda. "Path to Top Job Now Twists and Turns." *The Wall Street Journal,* March 15, 1993.
Berglas, Dr. Steven. *The Success Syndrome.* New York: Plenum, 1986.
Boldt, Laurence G. *Zen and the Art of Making a Living.* New York: Penguin Books, 1993.
Brady, John. *The Craft of Interviewing.* New York: Vintage Books, 1976.
Capell, Perri. "Special Report: Interim Executive Jobs." *National Business Employment Weekly,* 1993.
Carson, Richard D. *Taming Your Gremlin.* New York: Harper & Row, 1983.
Carter, Bill. *The Late Shift: Letterman, Leno, and the Network Battle for the Night.* New York: Hyperion, 1994.
Chu, Paul, and Jason Forsyth. "Brainstorm." *Success,* October 1993.
Coelho, Paulo. *The Alchemist.* New York: Harper San Francisco, 1993.
Covey, Stephen R. *The Seven Habits of Highly Effective People.* New York: Simon & Schuster, 1989.
Cowan, John. *Small Decencies.* New York: HarperBusiness, 1992.
———. *The Common Table.* New York: HarperBusiness, 1993.
Crowther, Karmen. *Researching Your Way to a New Job.* New York: John Wiley, 1993.
Davidson, Jeffrey P. *Blow Your Own Horn.* New York: AMACOM, 1987.
Dynerman, Susan Bacon, and Lynn O'Rourke Hayes. *The Best Jobs in America for Parents Who Want Careers and Time for Children Too.* New York: First Ballantine Books, 1992.
"Employment Market Survey: Summer 1993." Raleigh, N.C.: Employment Management Association.
Feingold, Dr. S. Norman, and Maxine H. Atwater. *New Emerging Careers:*

Today, Tomorrow and in the 21st Century. Garrett Park, Md.: Garrett Park Press, 1988.

Feingold, Dr. S. Norman, and Dr. Leonard G. Perlman. *Making It on Your Own*. Herndon, Va.: Acropolis Books, Ltd., 1991.

Garvin, David A. "Building a Learning Organization." *Harvard Business Review*, July-August 1993.

Gilette, Jay. "Lone Eagles Soar in the New Economy." *Points West Chronicle*, Winter 1992-1993.

Goldberg, Robert, and Gerald Jay Goldberg. *Anchors: Brokaw, Jennings, Rather and the Evening News*. New York: Birch Lane Press, 1990.

Great "Quotes" from Great Women. Lombard, Ill.: Celebrating Excellence, 1991.

Grunstra, Neal S. "More Professionals Find Temp Work Pays Off." *Washington Business Journal*, June 11-17, 1993.

Gutteridge, Thomas G., Zandy B. Leibowitz, and Jane E. Shore. *Organizational Career Development*. San Francisco: Jossey-Bass, 1993.

Handy, Charles. *The Age of Unreason*. Boston: Harvard Business School Press, 1989.

Hayes, Thomas C. "Faltering Companies Seek Outsiders." *The New York Times*, January 18, 1993.

Helgesen, Sally. *The Female Advantage*. New York: Doubleday/Currency, 1990.

Hill, Napoleon. *Think and Grow Rich*. New York: Fawcett Crest, 1960.

Hines, Andy. "Transferable Skills Land Future Jobs." *HR Magazine*, April 1993.

Hollandsworth, Skip. "Singing about Her Generation." *USA Weekend*, September 24-26, 1993.

HR Update. *HR Magazine*, November 1992.

Inc. Magazine 1994 Guide to Office Technology.

Insider's Guide to Law Firms, 1993-1994. Boston: Mobius Press, 1993.

"Job Search Still Changing." *HR News/Society for Human Resource Management*, August 1993.

Kimbro, Dennis, and Napoleon Hill. *Think and Grow Rich: A Black Choice*. New York: Fawcett Crest/Ballantine Books, 1991.

King, William B., Dean Graber, and Rebecca Newton. *Career Alternatives for Bankers*. Nashville, Tenn.: Magellan Press, 1992.

Koonce, Richard. "Taking Charge." *Executive Update*, April 1990.

Lerner, Rozelle. *Affirmations for the Inner Child*. Deerfield Beach, Fl.: Health Communications, 1990.

Martz, Sandra, ed. *When I Am an Old Woman I Shall Wear Purple*. Watsonville, Calif.: Papier-Mache Press, 1987.

McAdam, Terry W. *Careers in the Nonprofit Sector.* Washington, D.C.: Taft Group, 1986.

McGee-Cooper, Ann. *You Don't Have to Go Home From Work Exhausted!* New York: Bantam Books, 1992.

McNaught, Brian. *Gay Issues in the Workplace.* New York: St. Martin's Press, 1993.

Moran, Richard A. *Never Confuse a Memo with Reality.* New York: HarperBusiness, 1993.

Murphy, Kevin J. *Effective Listening: Your Key to Career Success.* New York: Bantam Books, 1989.

National Trade and Professional Associations of the United States. Washington, D.C.: Columbia Books, 1991.

Overman, Stephenie. "Not the Usual 9-to-5." *HR Magazine,* January 1993.

Perelman, Lewis J. *School's Out: Hyperlearning, The New Technology, and the End of Education.* New York: William Morrow, 1992.

"A Report on the Glass Ceiling Initiative." U.S. Department of Labor, 1991.

RoAne, Susan. *How to Work a Room.* New York: Warner Books, 1989.

Robbins, Anthony. *Awaken the Giant Within.* New York: Simon & Schuster, 1991.

Robinson, Bryan E. *Work Addiction.* Deerfield Beach, Fl.: Health Communications, 1989.

Rosen, Robert H. *The Healthy Company.* New York: Jeremy P. Tarcher/Perigee Books, 1991.

Sacharov, Al. *Offbeat Careers.* Berkeley, Calif.: Ten Speed Press, 1988.

Sabath, Ann Marie. *Business Etiquette in Brief.* Holbrook, Mass.: Bob Adams, 1993.

Sagan, Carl. *Broca's Brain.* New York: Ballantine Books, 1979.

Schepp, Brad. *The Telecommuter's Handbook.* New York: Pharos Books, 1990.

Schor, Juliet B. *The Overworked American.* New York: Basic Books, 1992.

Senge, Peter. *The Fifth Discipline.* New York: Doubleday Currency, 1990.

"Seven Trends That Will Change Your Future Worklife." *Personnel News,* May 1993.

Sher, Barbara. *Wishcraft.* New York: Ballantine Books, 1979.

Shields, Leslie, and Cydney Shields. *Work Sister Work.* New York: Simon & Schuster, 1994.

Silcox, Gordon B. "Employee Career Renewal: An Organizational Priority?" *HR Horizons,* Autumn 1992.

Sinetar, Marsha. *Do What You Love, The Money Will Follow.* New York: Dell, 1987.

———. *Living Happily Ever After*. New York: Dell, 1990.

"A Survey of Management Practices During Transition." Atlanta, Ga.: EnterChange, 1992.

Tanenbaum, Nat. *The Career Seekers*. Atlanta: Working Press, 1988.

Thurow, Lester. *Head to Head: The Coming Economic Battle Among Japan, Europe, and America*. New York: Warner Books, 1993.

von Oech, Roger. *A Whack on the Side of the Head*. New York: Warner Books, 1990.

Walters, Barbara. *How to Talk With Practically Anybody About Practically Anything*. Garden City, N.Y.: Doubleday, 1970.

Williamson, Alistair D. "Is This the Right Time to Come Out?" *Harvard Business Review*, July-August 1993.

Yeager, Neil M. *CareerMap: Deciding What You Want, Getting It, and Keeping It!* New York: John Wiley, 1988.

Index

Abbott, Jim, 22
accountability, 34
acting, as career, 25–26
action plan, *see* career action plan
affirmations, career, 15
Affirmations for the Inner Child (Lerner), 8n.
age, and success, 10
Age of Unreason, The (Handy), 129
Alchemist, The (Coehlo), 159
Alexander, Jane, 39, 101
alliances, forming, 36
American Society of Association Executives, 103
America Online, 140
Anchors: Brokaw, Jennings, Rather and the Evening News (Goldberg and Goldberg), 145
Anderson, John, 21n.
Apple Computer, 9, 89
Association of Part-Time Professionals (APTP), 104
associations, 101–103, 124–125

banking industry, 80
Barker, Bob, 105
Bennis, Warren, 1
Berglas, Steven, on success, 17–18
Blow Your Own Horn (Davidson), 36
"borderless" jobs, 3
boss
 as budget slasher, 74–75
 characteristics of, 65–71
 and mentoring, 13, 62, 127–128
 see also CEOs

Brady, Jim, 144
Brady, Sarah, 144
Brice, Fanny, on identity, 8
Buchwald, Art, 128
Bushnell, Nolan, on interdisciplinary approach, 147–148
business process reengineering (BPR), 35

Campbell, Joseph, 126
Capability Corporation, 59
Capell, Perri, 99–100
career action plan, 56–60
 creating, 58–59
 moving from goals to, 57–58
career affirmations, 15
Career Alternatives for Bankers (King, Graber, and Newton), 80
career change, "talking points" in, 111
career goals
 believing in, 52–55
 and characteristics of boss, 65–71
 establishing, 11, 50–52
 examples of, 59–60
 failure to achieve, 46–48
 moving to action plan from, 57–58
 pursuing, 55–56
 and rites of passage, 12
career gremlins, 133
career paths, 2–3
career planning, as process, 21
Career Search, 60
Carpenter, Mary Chapin, 125–126
Carson, Richard, on career gremlins, 4

Carter, Bill, on focus, 48–49
CEOs
  and downsizing, 32
  nonprofit, 102
  see also boss
change, 129–137
  adapting to, 135–137
  career, "talking points" in, 111
  communication and, 134–135
  as a constant, 2, 13, 30
  coping with, 131–135
  as focus of work, 36
  job, 35
  warning signs of, 74–75
charity work, 157–158
Charles, Ray, 22
Cleese, John, 39
Clinton, Bill, 10
co-creating jobs, 100–101, 118
codependency, 8, 47
Coehlo, Paulo, 159
comfort zone, stepping out of, 19, 143
communication, and change, 134–135
CompuServe, 140
computers
  impact on world of work, 3, 33, 35, 89–90, 104
  and information superhighway, 136
  in lifelong learning, 139–141
consultants, 91, 94–95
contracts
  consulting, 94
  employment, 97
  self-employment, 92
control freaks, 69–70
Coolidge, Calvin, on persistence, 55
core competencies, 34
core employees, 2
Cowan, John
  on accomplishments, 43–44
  on in-depth knowledge, 30
Crannell, Mary, on attitudes and success, 26–27
Crowther, Karmen, 80
cumulation, law of, 21–23, 48–49
curiosity, 147

Davidson, Jeffrey, 36
DeBolt, Don, 124–125
DeBruhl, Mike, on Professional Profile statements, 81
Delphi, 140
development, *see* professional development
diet, 154
Dillon, Rick, on creating opportunities, 53–54
diversity, cultivating, 146–147
Domino's Pizza, 9
Do What You Love, The Money Will Follow (Sinetar), 1
Downs, Hugh, 152
downsizing, 32, 106–107
  feelings about, experiencing, 78
  signs of pending, 74–75
dress, for job interviews, 114
Dubois, W. E. B., on satisfaction in work, 151

eating habits, 154
economy, U.S.
  changes in, 2
  employment arrangements in, 3
Edison, Thomas, on ideas, 147
education
  lack of, 9
  see also lifelong learning; professional development
Einstein, Albert, 9
Emerson, Ralph Waldo
  on success, 17
  on use of time, 61
Employee Assistance Program (EAP), 134
employee benefits, and temporary employment, 99
employee development, *see* lifelong learning; professional development
employment contracts, 97
Employment Management Association, 33
EnterChange, Inc., 134–135

entrepreneurship, 24, 90–93
  and consultants, 91, 94–95
  of family-run businesses, 97–98
  of home-based businesses, 90–93, 140
  of start-up companies, 79, 96–97
Everhart, George, 89
Executive Recruiter News, 100
Executrack, Inc., 84
exercise, 135, 153–154
expectations
  and "good employee" syndrome, 49–52
  of others, 6–8, 18, 49–52
  positive, 158–159
experience
  defining, 40–45
  leveraging, 38–39, 144–145
  in synergy of skills and talents, 39–40
external résumé, 72, 80–88

family of choice, 157
family-run businesses, 97–98
family scripts, 7–8
fear, accepting, 12
"fear of success" syndrome, 52
feelings
  experiencing, 78
  expressing, 133–134
Feingold, Norman, 93
Fifth Discipline, The (Senge), 30
first impressions, 114
focus, in attaining vision, 48–49
franchising, 24–25, 95–96
friendship, 156–157

Garvin, David, on "learning organization," 32
Gay Issues in the Workplace (McNaught), 64
gays and lesbians, 64
Gillespie, Dizzy, 9
glass ceiling, 63, 123
goals, *see* career goals
"Going Through Focus" Technique, 19–20, 40–45, 51, 107–108
Goldberg, Jay, 145

Goldberg, Robert, 145
"good employee" syndrome, 49–52
Graber, Dean, 80
Greater Washington Society of Association Executives, 103
Growing a Business (Hawken), 93

hands-on management, 33, 34
Handy, Charles, on change, 129
Hawken, Paul, 93
Hawking, Stephen, 22
Head to Head (Thurow), 31
Hemingway, Ernest, 39
High Technology Marketplace Database and Fax-on-Demand, 60
Hill, Napoleon, on adversity, 16
holidays, networking and, 119
home-based businesses, 90–93, 140
Hower, Kathy, on power-oriented bosses, 69
humor, 158
Hutton, Lauren, 10
Huxley, Thomas, on action, 46

identity, *see* professional identity
Inc. Magazine's 1994 Guide to Office Technology, 89
incompetent bosses, 71
independent contractors, 91–93
industry trends, 62–63
informational interviews, 108–112
  asking questions in, 109–110
  inside information in, 110
  self-presentation in, 110–112
  "talking points" in, 110–112
Insider's Guide to Law Firms, The, 80
intentionality, 15–16
interdisciplinary approach, 147–148
interim employment opportunities, 98–100
internal job market, 72, 75–77
internal résumé, 72
International Franchise Association, 96
interviews, *see* informational interviews; job interviews

inventing careers, 122–128
    examples of, 122–126
    mentors in, 127–128
    rewards and risks of, 126–128

James, William, 12
jargon, in résumés, 84–86
Jennings, Peter, 9, 145
job goals, *see* career goals
job interviews, 109, 112–117
    and co-creating jobs, 100–101, 118
    etiquette for, 113–116
    evaluating "fit and feel" of job in, 117–118
    internal company, 75–77
    résumés in, 113, 114
    self-presentation in, 112–113
    and thank-you notes, 115
    warning signs in, 116–117
job market
    alternatives in, 89–104
    external, 78–88
    information about, 59–60, 79–80, 140–142
    internal, 72, 75–77
    and résumés, 72, 80–88, 108, 113, 114
Jobs, Steve, 9
job security, 2, 71–74, 106
job titles, 85–86
Johnson, Bob, on accomplishments, 84

King, William, 80
knowledge workers, 31, 35, 90
Kraus, Roberta, 21n.

Late Shift, The (Carter), 48–49
law, 80
law of cumulation, 21–23, 48–49
Lear, Bill, 9
learning, 134
    see also lifelong learning; professional development
Leary, Timothy, 105
leaves of absence, 145–146
Leno, Jay, 48–49
Lerner, Rozelle, on family scripts, 7–8

lesbians and gays, 64
lifelong learning, 138–151
    in current job, 143
    and finding meaning in work, 149–151
    high-tech vs. low-tech approaches to, 139–143
    interdisciplinary approach in, 147–148
    and leveraging personal experience, 38–39, 144–145
    "mental health" breaks in, 148–149
    networking in, 142–143, 146–147
    sabbaticals in, 145–146
    see also professional development
Living Happily Ever After (Sinetar), 152
Lloyd George, David, 122
"lone eagles," 90
Lucht, John, on job changes, 35
Lynch, Pat, on cutting-edge skills, 32

magazines, 59–60, 79–80, 141–142, 148–149
Mailboxes, Etc., 96
Making It On Your Own (Feingold and Perlman), 93
Managhan, Tom, 9
May, Rollo
    on absorption in work, 150
    on self-limitation, 9
McDonald's, 96
McNaught, Brian, 64
meaning, in work, 58, 149–151
men
    and expression of feelings, 133–134
    and friendship, 156–157
"mental health" breaks, 148–149
mentors, 13, 62, 127–128
Michener, James, 10
micromanagement, 69–70
miniaturization, 35
minority groups, and glass ceiling, 63, 123
mission, career, 58, 149–151
"moments of glory," 40–45, 82
motivation, 113

Index

moving up, "talking points" in, 111–112
multiculturalism, 146–147

National Business Employment Weekly, The, 79, 99–100
networking, 69, 70, 71, 72–73, 76, 105–121
   and consulting, 94
   effects of, 118–119
   "Going Through Focus" technique in, 107–108
   at holiday times, 119
   importance of, 106–107
   informational interviews in, 108–112
   in inventing careers, 127–128
   job interviews in, 109, 112–117
   in lifelong learning, 142–143, 146–147
   making connections in, 107–108
New Complete Guide to Environmental Careers, The, 80
Newton, Rebecca, 80
Niebuhr, Reinhold, on serenity, 135
nonprofit organizations, 101–103, 124–125, 157–158

Organizational Development (Shore), 34
organizations
   developing knowledge of, 62
   and industry trends, 62–63
   nonprofit, 101–103, 124–125, 157–158
   values of, 64–65
Overworked American, The (Schor), 132

parent-child relationships, at work, 8–9, 69
part-time employment, 103–104
Peale, Norman Vincent, on problems, 153
Pederson, Laura, 10
Perelman, Lewis, 140
performance reviews
   preparing for, 72
   shifts in, 75
Perlman, Leonard, 93
persistence, 55–56

Peters, Tom, on consultant's mind-set, 72
Phillip Morris, 78
Pomeroy, Bradley, 122
positioning, in job-hunting, 119–120, 121
positive expectation, 158–159
Powell, Colin, 10
power, boss's focus on, 69
presentation skills, 143, 144
procrastination, 5–6
Prodigy, 140
professional development
   employer commitment to, 65
   importance of, 3
   job changes in, 35
   lifelong learning in, 138–151
   networking in, 142–143, 146–147
   personal commitment to, 74
   see also lifelong learning
professional identity
   and career "boxes," 13, 14–15
   developing, 13
promotion, prospects for, 63–64
Prospect Associates, 65
public speaking skills, 143, 144

questions
   informational interview, 109–110
   internal interview, 76–77
   job interview, 114
   of self, 20–21

Raphael, Sally Jesse, 22–23
Reagan, Ronald, 39
references, 81, 86–88
rehiring process, 113
Researching Your Way to a Good Job (Crowther), 80
responsibility, for career, 1–16
   barriers to, 4–11
   and consultant's mind-set, 72
   tips for assuming, 11–16
   and trends in workplace, 1–4
résumés
   "broadcast" campaign with, 108

résumés (*continued*)
    external, 72, 80–88
    internal, 72
    and job interviews, 113, 114
rewards, 135
rising stars, 73
Rites of Passage at $100,000 (Lucht), 35
Robbins, Anthony, 10
    on luck, 78
    on quality of questions, 20
    on thinking big, 5
Robinson, Bryan, 155
Robinson, Kevin, on adversity, 10–11
Roddenberry, Gene, 22
Rodland, Jack, 156–157
Rogers, Carl, on educated person, 131
Roosevelt, Eleanor, on adversity, 12–13

sabbaticals, 145–146
Sagan, Carl, on Einstein, 9
Sanders, Harland, 105
satisfaction, job, 149–151
Schepp, Brad, 104
School's Out (Perelman), 140
Schor, Juliet, 132
Schweitzer, Albert, on serving others, 158
self-confidence, 113
self-doubts, 4–5
self-employment, 91–95
self-limitations, 9
self-presentation, 112–113
Senge, Peter, 30
serenity, 135
serving others, 157–158
sexual orientation, 64
Shaw, George Bernard, on success, 16
Sher, Barbara
    on brainstorming, 19
    on fear, 89
    on negative thinking, 133
    on networking, 105
Shields, Cydney, 64
Shields, Leslie, 64, 123
Shissai, 158
Shore, Jane, on core competencies, 34

short-term job performance, 2
Sinetar, Marsha
    on choosing a career, 1
    on happiness, 152
skill-set, 30–45
    as asset, 3
    creating job pathways with, 36–39
    defining, 40–45
    and "moments of glory," 40–45, 82
    in synergy of talents and experience, 39–40
    transferring to nonprofit sector, 103
    trends concerning, 32–36
    updating, 3, 32–33
Small Business Administration (SBA), 92–93
Small Decencies (Cowan), 30, 43–44
Smith, Howard K., 105
solitary time, 148–149, 154–156
start-up companies, 79, 96–97
Stephanopoulous, George, 10
strategy, career, 11
Street Smart Career Guide (Pederson), 10
stress
    and change, 132–134
    and exercise, 153–154
    managing, 152–153
    and support system, 134
success, 17–29
    and age, 10
    attitude toward, 9–11
    in current job, 61–77, 143–146
    expanding options for, 23–27
    "Going Through Focus" technique and, 19–20, 40–45, 51, 107–108
    and law of cumulation, 21–23, 48–49
    personal definition of, 17–19, 27–29
    questions of self and, 20–21
Success Syndrome, The (Berglas), 17–18
support staff, 73–74
support system
    and change, 133–134
    family of choice in, 157
    friendships in, 156–157

talents, 36
    defining, 40–45
    in synergy of skills and experience, 39–40
Taming Your Gremlin: A Guide to Enjoying Yourself (Carson), 4
taxes, and home-based businesses, 91–92
technology
    advances in, 3, 33, 35, 89–90, 104
    information management, 137
    and lifelong learning, 139–141
Telecommuter's Handbook, The (Schepp), 104
telecommuting, 104
temporary employment, 98–100
thank-you notes, 115
Thoreau, Henry David, 18
    on focus, 6
Thurow, Lester, on brainpower industries, 31
Total Quality Management (TQM), 35
training, *see* professional development
transfers, 143
twelve-step programs, 135

upward mobility, 33

vacation, 155, 156
value-added contribution, 34
values, 64–65
victim mentality, 13
"virtual" work options, 3
vision
    career action plan in, 56–60
    career goals in, 46–56, 59–60
    defined, 58
    focus in, 48–49
    and "good employee" syndrome, 49–52
visualization, 11
voices, internal, 4–5
volunteer activities, 157–158

Wambaugh, Joseph, 39
warning signs, of change, 74–75
Whalen, Matt, on serenity, 70
Wishcraft (Sher), 19, 89
women
    and glass ceiling, 63, 123
    and vicarious living, 47
work addiction, 155
Work Sister Work (Shields and Shields), 64, 123
work style, 52–53, 64–65
Worley, Bob, 46, 142